The Parental 411 – What Every Parent Should Know about Their Child in College

Dr. Boyce D. Watkins
www.boycewatkins.com

Blue Boy Publishing Co.
Camillus, NY.

Published by

Blue Boy Publishing Co.
PO Box 691
Camillus, NY. 13031 – 0691

Printed in the United States of America

First printing, July, 2004

ISBN: 0-9742632-3-0

Cover designed by Jonathan Gullery.

For more information on speaking engagements or questions, please go to the author's website at www.boycewatkins.com. You may also send email to info@boycewatkins.com

Other titles by Dr. Boyce Watkins

www.boycewatkins.com

Everything You Ever Wanted to Know about College – A Guide for Minority Students

Quick and Dirty Secrets of College Success – A Professor Tells it All

To request large quantities for classes or seminars, please contact the publisher directly at the address above. You can also call (315) 487-1176 or email info@boycewatkins.com. There are substantial discounts for orders of 50 books or more.

To request Dr. Watkins as a speaker, please also use the contact information mentioned above.

787678

Dedication

To my daughter Patrice. This is also dedicated to Carmen, Charles, David, Diana, Dominique, Donald, Felicia, Lakisha, Larry, Latanja, Lawrence, Miya, Monique, Robin, Thaiiesha, and Valeria. I appreciate all the love and support they have given me, for this has made all the difference.

Table of Contents

vii

Why I Am Writing This Book

Although I have a child, I am not writing this book as a parent. I am going to leave the parenting up to you. I am writing this book as a professor, a student and a son.

As a professor, I can tell you what your kids are doing on campus. I can tell you how things work here, and I can tell you what is going on with your kids when you are not looking. If your child or children are anything like my own, you know that what they tell you is not always the entire story. So, in that regard, you can consider me a spy....a good spy, but a spy nonetheless. I consider what I do to be an important function in helping the parent and child work together to achieve success when the child goes off to college.

I am also someone who can tell you how the university works. I can give you the professor's perspective on what the best students do, how to deal with professors that cause you problems, and how to deal with the university as a whole. I can tell you what the university is thinking when they deal with your child, or what the football coach is most interested in when he shows up on your front porch during the recruiting trip.

I have taught thousands of students over the years, befriended them, jumped on their case when they went astray, and had many of them cry in my office when things weren't going so well. So, I guess you can say, as a professor, I have seen it all. As a young professor, I also have the ability to relate to students in ways that their parents cannot. I began teaching at the college level shortly after my 22nd birthday. In fact, half my class was older than I was! I watch the same TV shows, listen to the same music, play basketball with students, and I even thought about joining the break dancing team on my campus. I mention all this to say that students are very likely to relate to me in ways that they don't expect to relate to professors. In fact, I have more in common with the students than with my colleagues, many of whom are older than my parents. Having this connection helps me to understand the student better, and I can use this understanding to help you see things from your child's point of view.

As a student, I spent my standard 4 years in college, plus many years in graduate school. My mother, like you, was my greatest ally as I went through the horrific struggles of obtaining a PhD. No one in my family had ever gone to graduate school, at least not long enough to complete a degree. So, traveling these uncharted waters was an intimidating and downright frightening experience. The emotional and social baggage that I picked up along the way has kept me up at night, and although the process was strengthening and rewarding, it was, in some ways, psychologically damaging.

Your role as the parent is critical to the success of your child. The key, however is that your role be tempered with the desire to help your child learn and grow through the process. This means knowing the delicate balance between stepping in and flowing out. You do not want to come in like troops in Iraq, occupying your child's life like the military. You want to provide tangential support, with a clear phase-out plan so that your child can eventually obtain independence in his/her life. That is a tough role for parents, which is what makes this process so difficult.

As a son, I can tell you about the things that my own parents did that created the right incentives, and some things they did to create the wrong incentives. I recall spending many months angry at my parents for things that they did for my own good. I can also think of times when they might have done things better, had they known the recipe. But the key is that if, in the end, the good outweighs the bad, then you have won the game. Just like in basketball, sometimes you give up points and sometimes you score them. What matters is that you score more than you give away.

My parents were, for the most part, successful when it came to raising their children and getting us through the educational system. My sister is on her way through medical school, my brother is nearing college graduation as an engineering student, and of several hundred graduates, I was the only African-American in the world (that I know of) to earn a PhD in Finance during the year of my graduation. I would have to admit that these were proud achievements for my parents. But most of us know that anything worth having is going to be very difficult to obtain. So, as much as I would like to say that the path was smooth, it was not. In fact, there were days when it was horrible. To know that we made it through the storm to the end of the tunnel is a blessed feeling indeed.

All of these views (professor, student and son) can provide potentially insightful perspectives that are designed to help you do your job more effectively. There are times when outside observers can help us gain insight into ourselves that we never knew existed. It works the same as a camera. When I was a runner, I had one perspective. I could feel myself running and see my opponents. But my coaches would tell me that I wasn't lifting my knees high enough. It was not until my coach showed me videotape of my mistakes that I realized what I needed to do. Also, when my opponents told me that they were able to pass me at the end of the race because I slowed down, that also gave me insights I did not have. So, hopefully, as you go through the tangled web of parenting, these additional insights from a professor, student and son will add to the set of information that you can put in your pocket and use when you find yourself confronted with challenging and intense situations.

One other thing to remember is that this is a dual effort process. Both the parent and child must be informed and prepared to do what is necessary to be successful at the college level. If your child wants to read more about how they can become prepared for college, they can read one of my other books: *Quick and Dirty Secrets of College Success – A Professor Tells it All* or *Everything You Ever Wanted to Know About College – A Guide for Minority Students.* Both of these books give the inside scoop for college students on how to prepare for college and succeed when they get there. The guide for minority students is not just for minorities, however. Most of the information students need is universal, since the struggles of college do not change with the ethnicity of the individual.

How Do Our Lives Become Such a Darn Mess?

"When I screwed up in college, I had no idea that I was starting the process for screwing up my life. I wish that I could do it all over again." – Anonymous ex-student (all quotes are anonymous)

I would not say I am a pessimist when it comes to students and their performance on college campuses. I can only say that my feelings are hurt on a daily and weekly basis. Being a college professor is a great job. However, one of the psychologically challenging aspects of this position is that you are continuously getting older and wiser, while your partners in the process (the students) are staying the same age and making the same mistakes. Imagine having a best friend and when they are 20, you are 20. Then, when you are 30, they are 20. When you are 50, they are 20. As you get wiser, they continue to make the same mistakes and see the world as a 20-year old. When you were young, you could deal with the mistakes and immaturity. But as you get older, you find yourself ready to bang your head through a brick wall. You feel bad for your friend, for he/she seems to be making no progress. Because you care about them, you hate seeing them go through the same tragedies over and over again.

That is how I feel when dealing with students. Every year, you know that students are going to make the same mistakes as the students before them. You know that so many students are going to flunk out. You know that so many students are going to die of alcohol poisoning. You know that so many students are going to get raped, hooked on drugs, commit suicide or become alcoholics. Try as you might, you find that there is no progress being made, and each year, you see that the world is no different from the one that you saw the year before.

While this problem cannot be easily solved, writing this book and sharing this information with you is my small effort to combat this problem. Many parents are not aware of these issues, and they only find out about the problem after little Jimmy has come back home to live with them at the age of 26. Jimmy comes home and then he doesn't leave, mainly because he has never learned to take care of himself. Planning for retirement and getting on with your life is going to be a lot tougher if you are serving as someone else's personal Welfare Office.

If one were to try to break down the problems that students run into in college, we could break them into two categories: 1) Social problems and the 2) Academic problems. Surprisingly, in my experience, the academic problems are not nearly as strong as the social ones. In fact, the academic problems are usually *symptoms* of the social problems, the same way that coughing is a symptom of having a cold. Basically, a student's success in college has a great deal to do with whether the child chooses to have the psychological make up necessary to do a job every day and show personal responsibility.

So, let's break down some of the problems, and as the book goes on, I am going to discuss solutions and things that parents can do to support their child through the process. One important thing I should say before discussing the problems is this: Your child has a certain amount of free will that serves as the critical factor in their success. You *cannot* force them to follow your advice, and you *cannot* control their lives. All you can do is provide advice and incentives, then hope they choose to do the right thing.

I will tell a story to illustrate the point I am making here:

I got a call from Jane, a mother who was concerned about her child's academic progress. Jane was a proud woman, one who took great pride in how her children were raised. She and her husband, a prominent attorney, had

19

done a wonderful job raising 3 incredibly intelligent, high achieving children. Of course, she was concerned to see her child not performing up to his potential. Being the high achiever and supportive mother that she was, it was difficult for her to not feel some responsibility for her son's problems. To solve the problem, Jane first helped her son get an off campus apartment so that he could focus more on his studies. She then started investigating her son's habits. She hired tutors and did everything she could to get her son's grades up. Nothing seemed to work.

So, I agreed to meet with her son and consult with him about his academic struggles. The meeting was easy and relaxing, since her son was a good kid and extremely intelligent. Also, I was careful not to tell her son what to do, but instead, to simply share my perspectives and offer to help if he was struggling. After talking to her son for an hour, I got a very good feel for the issue. Basically, her son, like myself, was big fan of Xbox videogames. As a freshman, I am not sure he was aware of research showing that students who play lots of videogames tend to have lower GPAs than those who do not. The issue is a simple one: given that time is money, if you are spending all your money on hamburgers and candy bars, you don't have any money to pay your rent. The analogy is that since he was spending 60 hours per week playing Xbox, there was no way he was going to have time to get all his homework done, especially as a Physics major.

My suggestion to the mother was to discuss the issue with her child, but to recognize the fact that he was no longer a baby. Although we can agree that few of us are wise at the age of 18, the fact was that she had to acknowledge that he was responsible for his own actions. Additionally, we all have different levels of tolerance when it comes to how many times we have to hit our head before we change our actions. Some people never change. Some don't need to hit their head at all. Some people have to be darn near dead before they realize that they should do some things differently. She had to, like all of us, accept the fact that her son may have to go through some struggles before he realizes that spending all his time on videogames might have a negative impact on his future.

What is the point of this story? It is not meant to say that either the mother or the child was doing anything wrong. It is to say that there is only so much we can do to change the actions of another person. Just like in the bible (in the event that you are religious), it is mentioned that while God can impact our lives in certain ways, he cannot impact our free will. This might be considered true for students.

The other side of this issue is the fact that we do have some control over what our kids do in college. The inability to directly impact someone's free will does not mean that we cannot create *strong incentives* for that person to change their actions. Some parents go too far to the extreme of not recognizing that they can have some impact on their child's choices. They assume that the child cannot be controlled, and they have no right to tell them what to do. I must differ with this viewpoint, since I was raised to believe that if someone else is paying your bills, then they have SOME RIGHT to tell you what to do. When you are financially, physically and emotionally independent of the person, it is at that point that they have no right to impact your life whatsoever.

My Parents – Fully Undressed

"Ya'll never did teachedided me." - *Boyce Watkins, age 5 in response to his mother asking him why he loaded the dishwasher the wrong way. .*

My parents were interesting people. When it came to raising their children (myself in particular), they often found themselves treading unfamiliar territory. My mother was a 16-year old high school junior when she found out that she was pregnant. I was born when she was 17. My biological father decided, for his own reasons, that he was too young for a family, so he was actually out of the picture earlier than I can even remember. I don't hate him for it, I just went on with my life. After hearing about his life in and out of prison, I am usually happy that he chose to do something else, since I could have easily ended up in the jail cell right next to him.

My mother married my "real father" when I was about 4 years old. They were both young parents, incredibly inexperienced. When I think back to their raising me at such an early age, I often wonder why we don't have laws against some parents having children too young. Maybe they should ship all of us little "Love Children" off to a farm to be raised by chickens, since there were times when my parents' child-rearing techniques left much to be desired.

The father that raised me was a good, hard-working man, but emotionally distant as well as strong and stern. I would like to have learned more from him over the years, but in hindsight, I am simply blessed and happy that he felt compelled to take care of a child that didn't belong to him. Sure, it helped that my mother was bombshell pretty, but I am sure that, like my biological father, he could have spent his time doing other things.

Through the years, I learned from my father mostly by watching him. He was a very tough man, mentally and physically. I learned the value of determination, hard work

24

and courage from seeing him overcome his own obstacles. He was a Vietnam Veteran, and the kind of person who seemed to be able to look every obstacle in the eye and dominate it immediately. I learned from him that most barriers in life are psychological, and if you are not confronting, challenging and defeating those barriers, then it is usually by your own choice. He always showed tremendous love, but primarily through actions, not words. In fact, he acted as though he barely knew that I had written my first book, but you can imagine my surprise when I came home and saw that he had framed it and placed it prominently in the living room. He was a living prototype of the value of tough love.

My mother, on the other hand, was the parent to which I was closest, mainly because she was the one that actually talked to me. She was also the one who dealt with the worst of me as I went through my teenage years, fighting her night and day over every little issue. She was the one that taught me about the value of having tremendous emotional passion, or being downright crazy when it came to getting what you want. I remember her telling me things like "If they tell you to arrive by 8 o'clock to get something, you should get there by 6", or "Being a minority means that you have to be twice as good at all times." Given that she was such a passionate and emotional person, this led to a lot of our conflicts as she herself was learning how to deal with a teenage boy. There were times when her parenting techniques only served to chastise my manhood, but that was all she knew.

My parents did not have the same kind of household that many of my friends and relatives had. Their rule was law, and there was no debate. My father made it very clear that his home was a dictatorship, not a Democracy. I can recall going to my grandmother's house and getting into trouble with my male cousins. We would all go to family court, but we would get different sentences. I felt that my cousins would get off with light charges from their parents, while I was practically castrated. I never understood the value of this kind of punishment, but I remember my grandfather telling my mother "Either you discipline your kids now and control the process, or you wait until the government does it when they are older. But if you wait and let the government do it, you will have no say whatsoever." As I got older and saw many of my male friends go to the wayside of society, I understood why my parents were so tough on me.

While my parents worked hard to maintain a strict household, they made a lot of mistakes. They were young, and I always joke that my parents and I grew up together. I actually remember being 5 years old and my mother being only 22. I remember going to high school and my friends saying that they wanted to go out on a date with my mom. I could have gotten into a lot of fights over this! I recall at times, feeling emotionally damaged by the difficult and challenging environment they created around me.

I got my first job when I was 12 years old, selling newspapers on the corner. Just standing there, waiting for people to give me 50 cents to buy a paper. My second job was selling candy door-to-door. Talk about a tough job! But one thing I noticed was that from the time I got my first job, my parents treated me like the Federal Government: "You are working now, so the welfare program is coming to an end". From the time I started working, I was told not to ask for financial contributions from my parents for nearly anything. I was not given school clothes anymore, and I even had to pay rent at the age of 14. Yes, that sounds terrible, and indeed it was. I even felt that it was downright abusive. Had I been one of these kids today, I would have surely called the child abuse hotline and tried to have my parents sent to the electric chair. Not the one that kills them, just one that would make their hair stand up.

Believe it or not, grades were not enforced in my parent's household. Of course, I don't recommend this policy, but I can tell you how things went in my home. Remember: it's not about doing everything right, it's about the good outweighing the bad. If I had Fs on my report card as a high school student, nothing happened. I am not sure why my parents took this policy, but I suspect that it was because they felt that I would eventually learn the consequences of my actions. But then again, it could have been because they were tired of checking my report card. I remember asking my mother if she would give me money for making good grades. She asked me why she should give me money to do something that I should want to do for myself already. After all, I would be the one hurt if I didn't make good grades, not her. I thought this was very cruel, since most of my friends had signed blockbuster deals with their parents and were richer than Donald Trump on report card day. Yes, I was jealous!

I can summarize the effects of my parents' methods for raising me. There were some good and bad effects. The bad effects were that I felt unloved. I didn't feel that my parents nurtured me the way that I would have liked, and I wondered if they cared if I lived or died. Of course, years later, I know that they actually did care. The other bad effect was that because grades were not enforced in my household, I spent a lot of time earning very bad ones. I could not see, for the life of me, why school was important, or what it could do for my future.

The good effects were that, at a very early age, I learned personal responsibility. Whether intentional or not (I suspect they did this on purpose), I learned to do things *because I wanted to do them*, not because someone forced me to do so. I learned that, in this world, most people do not care about you, so it is up to you to care enough about yourself to do what you need to do.

I also learned how to work hard for what I wanted. *Gut-wrenchingly hard.* I did not work hard academically, but I worked hard on my job and in sports, which eventually translated over to academics once I got to college. I didn't choose to work hard because I was getting a nice fat check from my parents at the end of the day, I did it because I knew that it was going to be good for me and my future.

Finally, I learned that when I make mistakes in my life, I was going to be the one held responsible. My parents, in all their peculiar genius, had instilled a powerful feedback mechanism between my actions and my outcomes. The system became autonomous in the sense that they didn't have to create consequences for my actions, the consequences arose on their own. When I chose not to work, I didn't have any new school clothes for that year. When I chose not to study, my grades were in the toilet. They didn't create the over-nurturing buffer that many parents create that gives their kids a false sense of security and a skewed perception of reality.

Like any extremely difficult process, I was broken down and eventually built back up. Once I got to college, I had a level of maturity and life understanding that dwarfed my fellow students. I was considered the "wise old man" of my campus, because when it came to the silliness of college, I had a "been there, done that" attitude. No, I never had to experiment with drugs or alcohol, but I knew that drinking until you passed out was just flat out stupid. My parents had taught me enough consequences for my actions that I knew that flunking out of school, committing illegal activities, or getting involved in unhealthy habits was going to cause problems for me.

As a finance professor, I spend a lot of time thinking about the relationship between risk and return, and how a person's perception of risk changes, depending on who is going to suffer the consequences. Many students see college and their choices the same way that some banks saw the Federal Government during the Savings and Loan Crisis of the early 90s. Basically, these banks took unnecessary risks with their money, mainly because they knew that if things didn't work out, the government was going to protect them. Insurance companies work through the same problem, as they figure out how to charge a premium that does not give the customer an incentive to take extraordinary risks, like leaving their car doors unlocked. In other words, they make the customer share in the pain of a tragedy in the event that things go wrong (where do you think deductibles come from?).

Because many students do not feel the pain or the brunt of their actions, many of them do things that are just flat out stupid. The parents, serving the role as the federal government, swoosh in and save the child, carrying them away from danger like Superman carrying the ever-unappreciative Lois Lane, who refuses to stop getting herself into trouble. Perhaps if Superman had let Lois hit her head a few times, she might have been more careful.

Upon high school graduation, I was given the following options from my father (they sound a bit tough, but you will get the point shortly): "You have 6 months after the age of 18 to get out of the house. You can go to college if you want (which was highly suggested), you can get a job, go to jail or run the street. Either way, it's your choice and you've got to leave this house." For Christmas during my Senior year, I received luggage as a gift. So, the message was very strong and direct. The umbilical chord was being cut, and it was made clear that I was now an adult.

During college, the trend continued with my parents. Through my entire 4 years of college, I received two checks from my mother: each for $25. I had been warned all through high school that if I did not get a scholarship to college, I would be stuck paying for it myself. My parents made good on their promise. I was, through the grace of God, able to eek out a tuition scholarship to the state university down the road. But this was not enough to pay all my expenses, including room, board and books, which was actually greater than the cost of tuition. So, ultimately, I spent my entire first semester between the classroom, studying long hours in the library and working 3 jobs. On top of that, I had a child during the first semester of my Freshman year. You can imagine how "thrilled" my mother was, given that she was a counselor with the Teenage Parent Program, an organization that works to prevent teen pregnancy.

All of these realities hitting me for the first time were incredibly challenging and frightening. It was downright difficult, and there were days when I felt extremely bitter that no one was there to help me. I went through many days feeling sorry for myself, but I eventually realized that there would be no one there to pick me up after my temper tantrum. Eventually, I decided that rather than wallowing in self-pity, I should confront my challenges head on. As a result of my efforts and the toughness my parents instilled

30

in me, I earned the first 4.0 grade point average of my life. I was the top student on the entire campus, and my academic success led to my getting tons of scholarships, so many that I was able to pay all of my expenses and still have thousands of dollars left over. The impact didn't just stop with me. Seeing my success as a college student inspired my sister and brother, both of whom went on to become top students at their universities. My brother ran for student body president of his campus and earned admission to a summer leadership program at Harvard University. My sister was the top biology student on her campus and the first student from her school to be admitted to the summer pre-medical program at Johns Hopkins University. She is now a medical student and just spent her summer in a pre-residency program at The Mayo Clinic. My siblings and I responded to the tough child rearing approach of my parents by learning strength, focus and responsibility. We learned that in this world, it is critical that a person embrace self-determination and self actualization, for if you do not, you are going to be left behind.

As I reflect on this experience, I realize that if my parents had made things easier for me, softened the blow, flew in like Superman to save me from myself, I would not have achieved what I did. By doing things for myself, I found out that I could actually have *more* money in my pocket than my friends who simply sat around waiting for their parent's welfare check to arrive. I learned time management, as I knew that I could not waste my time going to party after party, but instead, I had to balance my fun with hard work. Basically, I learned the things that many of us learn as adults, only at an earlier age. I also saved my parents a lot of grief, since they could have spent all their retirement savings sending me check after check, so that I could buy more kegs of beer. Instead, I got my money from the university and from the corporation I worked for. In the long run, the situation turned out to be a serious win-win for my parents, the university and myself.

My parents' amazing role in my becoming the person I am today required a tremendous amount of courage from them. It required them to have the guts to say "I don't care what everyone else is doing, this is how things are going to go for you." This led to a great deal of ostracism for them, even from other adults who felt that they were simply being mean. The idea of charging RENT to your 14-year old child? Geez! But what I respect them for the most is that they did not allow a desire to be my best friend cause them to do things that were going to be detrimental to my future. This takes me to one of my favorite stories:

There was a little boy who found a caterpillar on the way home from school. He decided to take the caterpillar home and build him a cage. Each day after school, he watched the caterpillar in his cocoon, waiting for something to happen. He had heard that caterpillars come out of cocoons and turn into beautiful butterflies. One day, the little boy saw the cocoon start to crack. Day after day, he would see the cocoon crack more and more, as the creature inside worked his way to the outside. The boy, feeling a sense of attachment and protection toward the little caterpillar, felt sorry for it. So, he took some scissors and snipped away at the cocoon, just enough to make it easier for the caterpillar to work his way out. What the boy did not know was that the difficult process of working `its way out of the shell was how the caterpillar releases chemicals into its wings, creating the beautiful colors of a butterfly. It is also through the struggle that the caterpillar's wings gain their strength so that it can soar through the sky. But because the boy had felt sorry for the caterpillar and made *things easy for it, the butterfly was never as beautiful as it was meant to be, and it never learned to fly.*

My parents forced me to endure a great deal at an early age. But in all their youth, they understood one important, fundamental fact about life: Without struggle, there is usually no progress. If you protect your child in a cocoon their entire lives, they will never grow into the beautiful butterflies they can become. The things my parents did for me when I was a child have given me the courage and toughness to overcome many obstacles in my life, both personal and professional. At the same time, I have many friends I knew as children who do nothing but slog along, complain about every little thing they go through, feel continuously defeated, and don't have the guts or persistence to keep trying when things get rough. It is the difference in our upbringings that leads to our different reactions, and to my parents I owe an eternal debt.

Breaking Down the Academic Problems

"A college student is the only person that can begin reading the first chapter for a test that occurs in 3 days and feel that they are getting an early start." – anonymous professor.

Remember what I said earlier, the academic problems are usually a symptom of social ones. This is ironic, given that college is supposedly about academics. But the thing about college is that rather than simply being a place to learn math, biology and English literature, it is also a place to learn about life. It is where we meet our best friends, have our most fun, and perhaps even meet the person that we are going to marry (or the person that we THOUGHT we were going to marry). I am going to discuss some of the common academic problems that students meet when going to college. I am going to propose solutions to these problems later in the book.

Cramming

Cramming is, in my opinion, the number one academic problem for college students. For some reason, people have an image of college being "The Great Cramfest". We see movies with footage of students spending all night in the library the night before the test, living off coffee and No-Doze. They come into the classroom the next morning like zombies from Michael Jackson's "Thriller" video. For some reason, they think that the hours of studying they did the night before is going to make up for the weeks of not studying that have already taken place.

This is not how college is supposed to work. First of all, cramming is usually not a good strategy, no matter what. Some students can get by with it, but these are also students that are likely to end up with ulcers at the end of their college career. Cramming is risky, stressful, addictive

36

and likely to fail. The greatest problem that many students have when it comes to succeeding in college is that they do not have the ability or maturity to know how to work consistently. The smart student learns early that an ounce of prevention is a ton of cure.

Lack of academic preparation

It can be frustrating to teach a class and see a student who doesn't seem to be prepared for the course you are teaching. As the professor, I am more frustrated for the student than I am for myself. Going into a tough Calculus or writing class and not having the skills to get through the course can be intimidating.

Fortunately, there are many ways to get around this problem. In fact, I would say that I would rather be a hard-working, unprepared student than a lazy student who has taken the course already. Nine times out of ten, the hard working student is the one that is going to end up on top.

Inconsistent study habits

A third academic problem that plagues many students is one of consistency in their study habits. Many students simply do not know how to study every day. This boggles my mind, since most of these same people know how to go to football practice every day, to work at McDonald's every day, or to call their boyfriend every day. But studying every day is something that is extremely difficult for most college students to do. I separate the consistency problem from the cramming problem, but in some ways, they are duals to one another: consistency keeps you from having to cram. But the ultimate question is "Why do students have a hard time studying consistently?"

Part of it has to do with the culture shock of being on campus. Basically, most students have never been in a situation in which they were not forced to do homework every single day. Homework keeps us disciplined. It forces us to face immediate consequences for our actions and it is easy for us to do something that is right in our face. The idea of spending every single day preparing for an exam at the end of the month is only something that the most disciplined person can do. This is where maturity comes in, since a disciplined individual is usually someone who has simply bumped their head enough times to know that if they are not focused, they are going to suffer. Most 18-year olds have not been forced to bump their heads, since they have been protected all their lives. Coming from good families with responsible parents, they were not forced to endure the hardships that come along with an undisciplined life.

What is saddest about the protective environments that children come from is that in some cases, the pain of reality has only been deferred. Life can be extremely hard on someone who has not been forced to confront the consequences of their actions. If a child has not been forced to endure consequences at an early age, they are going to endure them in a much harsher form later in life when the world shows how little it cares about that person. These lessons start in college, where the child meets some of the heartless professors who don't care if you've studied or not. They simply give you the grade you deserve and keep going. A child that is used to being nurtured is going to have a hard time dealing with this form of emotional detachment. The reality, however, is that professors have hundreds of students, and it is extremely difficult to find out why each student is or is not doing the work that they were told to do.

Most students, in their lack of study consistency, also do not visit their professors or seek out tutors early enough to help them make it through the course (I discuss tutors in more detail in the section on Supporting your Child Through Academic Hardship). Rather than getting a tutor before a difficult course begins, many students would rather wait until the week before the final exam, when they have a grade lower than the depths of hell. When I was a tutor in college, I was always overworked during finals week. Booking me during finals week was tougher than getting Brittany Spears during the Grammies. I would wonder why these same individuals had not called me earlier, back when I was sitting around twiddling my thumbs. I would also become irritated by the fact that they waited till the last minute, and then thought that because they paid me 15 dollars per hour, I was supposed to solve all their problems.

The late rushes continued as I became a professor. Every year, right before each exam, I always have students in my office trying to learn 6 week's worth of material in 2 hours. I admit that this can leave most professors both annoyed and frustrated. Given that I am extremely busy, my ability to sit and explain 6 weeks worth of material in two hours to one person (out of 200 that I teach in a semester) is extremely limited. The idea that there are students who think that it is the job of the professor to "feed" them the material is problematic. When a student expects to be spoon fed, it is usually the case that this student had things fed to him/her during high school. I then wonder if their parents have convinced the child that it is the job of the world to spoon-feed things to them. Either

39

way, I feel sorry for the child, since this is not the way the world works. It is not that helping the student is a problem for me, it's when the student has done nothing on their end to facilitate the process, and instead feels that I am the surrogate parent that is there to help them avoid the consequences for their actions.

Overconfidence and complacency

Before teaching Finance to college students, I taught mathematics. One of the classes I taught was Calculus I, the "weed-out" course for Engineering and Math majors. The class was so tough, even God's Angels would have come begging for a tutor! Sadly enough, we seemed to take some pleasure in really pushing the limits of students, not to be mean about it, but just to make sure that they were ready for the next level of academic Mathematics and Engineering. Some students would come into the class as math jocks and leave the class looking for any major they could find that had no math involved. I can't tell you how many people started off as Engineers, only to end up as Social Work and Philosophy majors after taking "Calc I".

One of the running jokes of the Math Department was about "The Student". Who was "The Student"? You would have one every semester. This was the person that came up to the professor on the first day of class, bright-eyed and bushy-tailed. They would say something like this: "Sir, I just wanted you to know that I've already taken this class in high school. In fact, I have already passed the exams that would have let me skip this course. So, I already know everything you are going to cover, I am just taking the class as a review, but I know that it will be easy for me."

Well, the joke was that "The Student" was the one who was probably going to have one of the worst grades in your course. The issue was very simple: because this student has underestimated your course, they were probably not going to put forth nearly as much effort as the others. As much as we might try to warn this person that their complacency could be a problem, the message usually fell on deaf ears. They were going to find out, the hard way, that college-level Calculus is simply not the same as high school Calculus: the problems are tougher, the class is more rigorous and demanding, and the teacher expects a much higher level of precision than most teachers will expect in high school.

The same way that a person who makes a lot of money is more likely to be the one with no money at the end of the day (because they waste it), the student with the greatest number of high school accolades is in grave danger of allowing complacency to cause him/her to make mistakes that lead to a downward spiral. There is a story that I mention in my book *Quick and Dirty Secrets of College Success* about a student who went through what I am describing above. I feel that the story is incredibly important and illustrative of many things that your child may go through, so I am going to repeat the story here:

I had a friend in college, lets call her Angela. She and I were very good friends as Freshmen, but I was not in her league. Angela had been in the "Who's who" of high school students, she had an incredibly high score on the ACT and SAT, and she had a 4.0 GPA during her Senior year, before enrolling at our university. She majored in some kind of complex type of biology that I never heard of, and said that after college, she would become a neurosurgeon. I fully expected her to reach her goals. She

41

was an incredibly focused and confident student, with the ability to reach the stars.

The first semester didn't go so well for Angela. I think that she thought she was going to do well in college just because high school had gone so well for her. After all, you would expect a Valedictorian to have no problem with the freshman year! She thought that because she was bright, she didn't have to study as hard as everyone else. I, on the other hand, had never made good grades, so I was scared to death. I studied as hard as I could, and got the first 4.0 GPA of my life. Angela's grades weren't bad, but this was the first time in her life she had to stare down at a report card full of Bs and Cs. She really didn't know how to take it.

One day, I saw Angela after class. She told me that she was going to move off campus, since it was cheaper. She also said that she was going to reduce her course load to about 2/3 of what it was before. I asked her why, and she said that it was because she felt that she could save money by moving away and taking fewer classes. Something didn't feel right, but I wasn't sure what it was. But being in support of my friend, I just gave her a hug and said "Good luck!"

I then started to see Angela less and less. I also noticed that when I would see her, something would always be different: maybe a new tattoo here or there, or she would seem to be smoking cigarettes or drinking more. She was still the same person in some ways, but in other ways, I could tell that she had lost her innocence. She no longer expected to make straight As, but had instead gotten used to seeing the little curly Cs and even some Ds on her report card.

She informed me about a year later that she was going to take a semester off from school. When I asked her why, she again said "To save money." I told her that I didn't think it was such a good idea, but she insisted that it was what she needed to do to "get her head together."

Eventually, I only saw Angela about once every six months. I would see her blond hair bobbing down the street toward my dorm, and I knew that she was coming to visit me. I was always happy to see her, but I worried about her. She was "kicking it" with the wrong people, and didn't seem too worried about studying. She had changed a great deal from the motivated student that she was when I met her.

Eventually, there came the day when Angela gave me the most interesting news of all: "I'm pregnant". For Angela, being pregnant meant that she was to go back home, at least that is what her parents told her to do. She wasn't in school anymore, and given that the father of her child had run off, there was really no reason for her to stay in town, away from her parents. So, she left to go home, where she stayed until after the baby was born.

I saw Angela again about 5 years later, when I was in graduate school. The baby had been born, a cute little child with chubby cheeks and blonde hair like his mother. She was now a full-time mom, and her days as an aspiring doctor were far behind her. She worked in a local fast food restaurant, and even as a 25 year old, still entertained dreams of becoming the doctor she once felt she was meant to be.

But life was different now. She was no longer a free-spirited 18-year old with her whole life in front of her. She was half way to 30, with a young child whose needs she had sworn to meet. Going to school was still possible, but

43

it would be much more difficult than before, which is why she never took the steps to go back. Essentially, her ability to reach those dreams had slipped away, and she was stuck with a life that she had not envisioned.

My friend's story is quite common on college campuses. You have many students who arrive to college without ever having experienced academic struggle. Many of these students, because they are so successful in the past, rely on their "tried and true" strategies of academic success, the same ones that they learned in high school. They find that since the terrain has changed a great deal, their ability to use the same old techniques and win battles with them is extremely limited. Therefore, when faced with a challenge, the student does not respond in a favorable way, and instead begins to accept outcomes that would have been unacceptable in the past.

Most successful people will probably say that the road to great success is typically paved with failure and devastation. What makes a person strong is not their ability to overcome obstacles, but rather, their ability to keep going when things are not going so well. Any doctor, lawyer or Indian Chief will tell you the same thing. Those students who respond to disappointment by giving up are those that are going to have the most trouble reaching their long-term academic goals.

Additionally, the over-achieving students are the ones who, many times, find themselves suicidal or using unhealthy coping mechanisms to make it through their struggles. I've seen students head to top law schools and resort to drinking to get over the stress of doing well on the LSAT. The pressure can sometimes come from the parent, who expects their child to be a world-beater, or simply nags their child into the ground every time they make a mistake.

Part of being a college parent is about understanding and realizing that your child is going to make some mistakes as part of their natural growth process. If you ride the waves with them and continue to give them constructive support, they will eventually find their way to success.

The Social Problems

"The drama of college makes a soap opera look like a boring version of Meet The Press" – anonymous college senior

In my experience, I've always felt that the social problems of college were the "whammy" that usually made the difference between the straight A student who goes on to medical school and the one who ends up in a medical facility for treatment. When I speak to students around the country, I usually start by telling them that college is a place of great opportunities. It is the opportunity to:

1) Get raped
2) Die from alcohol poisoning
3) Get addicted to drugs.
4) Catch a terrible venereal disease.
5) Obtain a gambling addiction.
6) Become a lifetime alcoholic.

The list really doesn't stop. I don't say these things to frighten the students, I say them to be realistic. I also say them to let students know that nearly everything in life as powerful as college is usually a double-edged sword. As we know, a double-edged sword can kill you or it can protect you from your enemies. It can also cut your food open or it can slit your neighbor's throat. How you use this weapon is up to you and the possibilities are simply endless.

In some ways, you could argue that the power of college is really too much for an 18-year old to handle. I don't agree with this assessment. I think that it is too much for an *immature and sheltered 18-year old to handle if they have not been trained with the right values.* A child that has never been forced to be responsible, and does not know how to do things in moderation is going to have trouble in college. The thing to remember, however, is that the age of 18 is a critical juncture in the child's life. If they do not go to college, they are going to be free to do *something*. In many ways, college is a good place to be, since being out in the street doing nothing is a quick recipe for disaster. A student with free time is going to use it, and if they are in a setting that encourages them to use that time for the wrong things, they are going to be in for a lot of trouble.

This reminds me of a consultation I had with a parent several years ago:

A mother and father were planning what to do with their child as she began her college career. She was turning 18, and leaving high school, a very bright girl with a high GPA and ACT score. Her parents felt that, although she was now 18, she was not emotionally prepared to start college. They then decided that she should not go to college for another year, and should instead stay home until her 19th birthday.

I did not agree with the parents' decision. I told them that, in my opinion, expecting your child to be mature before going to college was like expecting an athlete to be in shape before he/she begins training. The goal of training the athlete is to GET him/her into shape. In the same way, the goal of college is to take the immature student and allow that person to go through the life experiences necessary to breed maturity and responsibility that they would carry into adulthood.

The parents went against my advice, which was certainly within their rights. They felt that since they knew their child better than I did, they also had a better idea of what was best for her. I respected the decision, even though I made it clear that I did not agree. I eventually talked to the girl's parents about 8 years later, to find out how things turned out. The young girl had stayed in her home town for another year, but during that year, she got into all the things that we get involved with when are free to do what we want and when. She fell in love with a local guy that worked in a gas station, and got pregnant. Years later, she was still living in her home town, divorced from the guy in the gas station, but still taking care of his two children, for which he provides little or no financial support. In the end, the young lady with a world of potential suddenly found her world restricted to monthly welfare checks and working at the local grocery store.

This story was meant to illustrate the fact that sometimes as parents, we are too close to the situation to properly assess what is best for our kids. It's not that we make the wrong decisions, it's that we do not always do what is best for them in the long run. This is driven by the protective instinct we feel as parents. Watching our children struggle and suffer is not natural, so we can be tempted to avoid it at all costs. Also, as our child gets older, we still see them as the baby that they were many years ago. This reminds me of when OJ Simpson, after being accused of killing his wife and her male friend, was emotionally responsive to his mother whom, in spite of him being nearly 50 years old, was able to coddle him psychologically as if he were still in diapers. In fact, his mother was one of the catalysts that led to his surrender to police. The bond between parent and child can be an incredibly powerful thing, one that continues throughout the lives of all those involved.

The wonderland of college can be quite exciting. The interesting, and potentially dangerous thing about it is that no matter what you do when you are there, there is usually no one to reign you in if you get out of control. If your parents call and ask what you are doing, you can always construct a good lie. If your friends become suspicious of your activities, you can simply find new friends. There is always someone that you can hang out with that is interested in the same things that you want to do. If you want to smoke dope all day, you can find plenty of students to share the dope with you. If you play videogames all day, you will have lots of friends willing to do the same thing. I know kids that play videogames all day and all night on campus, longer than you can ever possibly imagine. I love videogames also, but being 12 years older than many of my students, I now understand the fact that playing the games for too long will eventually lead to my demise. Students do not yet understand some of these lessons.

I arrived on campus as a new father, having my child during the first semester of my freshman year. Also, I had never made good grades before. My high school grade point average was about 2.1, and I recall getting a D- in Senior English, which was just good enough for me to graduate. I didn't expect to survive in college, since it was pretty clear that I didn't have the same academic preparation as other students at the university.

But something happened during my freshman year. Having a child on the way really made me take my life more seriously. First, I realized that education was the key to creating a good future for my family and my daughter. Although her mother chose to do other things with her life, I knew that one day, when I was older, having an education would enhance my ability to take care of my child and provide her with the things she needed. So, I presumed that understanding "this college thing" might be enough to help me accomplish my goal.

Some of the approaches to child rearing used by my parents were downright mean, I agree. I was incredibly angry at my parents for quite some time, not even talking to my mother on some occasions. I felt that the harshness of my struggles were undeserved, since I was a good kid and a hard working student. However, this unique experience gave me a life perspective that my fellow students did not have. I knew that if I screwed up in school, I would be the one to bear the consequences. I knew that if I was arrested after a wild weekend party, I would be the only one of my friends who wasn't bailed out after the weekend was over. I knew that if didn't manage my time and money properly, the brunt of the problems created would fall on the guy named "Me".

As a result, I made different choices. I had as much fun in college as a person could have: I went to parties, played videogames, had a girlfriend and I played basketball with "my boys" on a regular basis. I had a wonderful time. At the same time, I built the professional and personal foundation for the rest of my life, and I am still receiving the benefits of good choices that I made back at that time.

I had many friends who were not so lucky. They got involved with things that seemed ok at the time, but were not. Maybe they pledged a fraternity and let their GPA slide. Maybe they got into trouble. Maybe they dropped out. But the sad thing is that anyone who has gone to college can think of at least 5 or 10 people (perhaps including themselves) who did not make the right choices and paid the price of a lifetime.

If I could summarize the categories of problems that students have when they come to campus, I would summarize them as follows:

Problems handling all the newfound freedom

Most students are dying to get out of their parents' house. The fresh relief of not having your parents there to tell you what to do is certainly something to live for. I know that I loved it, and you probably did too. But the danger for many students is that they take the freedom and run with it. Things are no longer done in moderation. Studying is done in lumps (if at all), partying is done by the keg-load, long nights at the frat house end up with vomit on the shoes and trips to the hospital. The things that we all might enjoy at some point in our lives are done in dangerous and potentially destructive quantities. While it is difficult to be prepared for this much freedom at the age of 18, there are things that parents can do to help their children become prepared.

The sad thing about all this freedom is that typically, it is the tough knocks of life that teach us the most. People talk about valuable lessons in their lives and the truth is that typically, that which is valuable is also costly. So, usually, our most valuable lessons were driven by our most costly experience. It is when you lost your last $200 that you learned to make sure that you kept your wallet in your front pocket. It was after a nasty and costly divorce that you learned the value of dating the right person. That is the way life works.

Students go through their hard knocks also, typically after doing things out of moderation. They eventually wake up and realize that they have not used their time productively and that the cost of their indiscretions was tremendous.

Not learning to manage their time

Students can be amazing when it comes to how incapable they can be at managing time. I am not sure where this comes from, but I suspect that many of them have simply not been placed into situations where they are forced to juggle multiple responsibilities. It reminds me of my own life. When I am in the middle of a busy semester, that is usually when I am forced to be productive. I know that wasting time is going to cost me dearly, since not completing important tasks on the job can get you into a lot of trouble. During my semesters of freedom, when I am not teaching, it is much more difficult for me to be productive. That is because I am tempted to say "Well, if I don't do it today, I can get it done tomorrow." This was not a good habit. So, eventually, I learned how to create deadlines for myself that keep me focused, even when there was nothing forcing me to do so.

Kids are the same way. Most students on my campus come from families that have the money to pay the $30,000 per year tuition bill. As a result, the parents usually have money to send their child every month, as if they are still 12 year olds needing an allowance. The parents seem to feel that this is their responsibility, and they tend to underestimate their child's ability to solve his/her own financial problems.

As a professor, I can tell you that while you might think that sending money to your child every week is going to give the child more time to study, it usually does not. What it does, in many cases, is gives your child more time for MTV, talking on the phone or going to parties. If a student wants to study, they are going to study, whether they have 40 hours of free time every week or 80. Keeping the child from having to get a job or do something that will cause him/her to use their time effectively is usually going to lead to results that are different from the ones that you've intended.

In fact, the students that come from the most humble backgrounds are usually the ones that show the most ability to manage their time. They work 15 – 20 hours per week, and they see their education as the way to reach their personal and financial goals. The worst student is the one that has their parents do everything for them and give them everything. It is almost as if the student is still wearing the diaper beneath their blue jeans. You feel for the child, for the child is not the one who is always to blame for the poor incentives that have been created in their life. Such students are not usually responsive when you force them to endure things that will cause them to be responsible. As a professor, it is very difficult to teach students who have not learned the value of personal responsibility. Even if everyone else in the class does well on a test, this is the person who still feels that it is someone else's fault that they received a failing grade. As a professor, this is sad to see.

Drugs, alcohol, gambling, sex and other collegiate vices

College has a lot of interesting traditions, some good and some bad. The age of 18 is a wonderful period in which you have a lot of "first times" that you remember for the rest of your life. What is bad about a lot of these college traditions is that many of them are downright unhealthy, particularly if done in excess. For example, many people (parents included) think that drinking excessively is simply something that college students do and that it is part of the tradition of college. What they don't remember is that many of the date rapes, deaths, assaults, car accidents and other unfortunate incidents usually occur with alcohol lurking in the background.

There was a student on one of the campuses on which I taught years ago. This person was a straight A student, headed to medical school after college. He was not a bad kid and actually well disciplined. One night, he and his friends got drunk behind the wheel. The student wrecked the car, killing the other driver and 3 of his best friends. He was arrested and sentenced to 15 years in prison. He was paroled 5 years later and worked hard to rebuild his life. One of his new life missions is speaking to college students about the dangers of alcohol on college campuses.

Because many kids have spent their lives in a vacuum created by their parents, the realities and dangers of college seem incredibly safe to them. They figure that if all the guys in their fraternity are drinking like pig fish, then they should also. After all, since when did our fraternity brothers ever steer us wrong?

Many students actually believe that they can drink heavily 4 days a week and NOT become alcoholics. How many people do YOU know that can drink a great deal and not eventually end up standing in front of a group of people at an Alcoholics Anonymous meeting? While drinking is an incredibly horrific collegiate vice, it is not the only one and perhaps not even the worst. There are many other kinds of poison that students can choose: gambling, drugs, and even sex. Aaaah, sex. One of the greatest extracurricular activities ever invented. As you also know, it is also one of the deadliest. Venereal diseases run rampant on college campuses. If you think about it, you can easily see why these diseases are so wide spread: a bunch of really horny kids with nothing to do except have sex with the same person that their best friend was having sex with last week. You can see how the cesspool gets yuckier by the second. Yes, sex is a natural and potentially beautiful thing, but it can be a terrible thing if not dealt with responsibly.

Surprisingly, gambling and videogame addictions are not as well documented or discussed as other types of addictions, primarily because they are in their earliest stages. Gambling is a huge growth industry, with Internet gambling coming on the scene. College campuses are full of students setting up gambling rings, and watching college basketball and football games with great intensity. What is also of interest is that students are sometimes incurring huge gambling debts. I recall reading a story about a college student who committed suicide because the "bookie" to whom he owed money had threatened to cut his mother's legs off if he didn't repay. So, needless to say, students have the ability to make a big mess of their lives and the lives of those they love.

Following the crowd

Peer pressure is one of the oldest and most powerful motivators known to man. It exists for newborn babies, 90 year olds, teenagers, and of course, college students. Many people do things without having a clue as to why they are doing them. All of us are guilty of this kind of thing.

But as we know, at different stages in our lives, we possess varying degrees of ability to do something that differs from the norm. It is now very easy for me to make decisions that others don't agree with, because they don't pay my bills and I don't care what they think. At the age of 18, maybe this was a tougher decision to make.

Many students have died on college campuses for following the crowd. I am usually saddened every fall when I hear about some freshman, going to her first major college party, who drank so much that her friends didn't know that she was dead at the end of the night. I can always see the promise in this student and what they might have been had they had the chance to live.

Some situations on campus increase the likelihood that students are going to be affected by peer pressure. For example, fraternities and sorority members, by definition, are those that tend to be influenced by those they are spending time with. They wear similar clothes, live together and make solemn pledges of lifelong brother/sisterhood. This is to be respected, for many of these bonds last a lifetime. However, there are times when these bonds get really messy. I had a student who "pledged" a fraternity that he badly wanted to join. The student was horribly abused, and nearly died after he was beaten for hours during his initiation. This is not an uncommon occurrence, as students get out of hand with the pledging process.

I've seen other students join fraternities and change into completely different people. Any group psychologist will tell you that the manner in which people behave in groups can many times differ dramatically from how they behave when they are alone. I have seen students come into college with very high GPAs, and extremely high aspirations, only to join the wrong group and head downhill. It's a really nasty process, and what is saddest about it is that the student has no idea that the transformation is taking place. For some students, it is their first time being accepted and belonging to a group. For others, it is a time when they are finding that their greatest fantasies are being fulfilled (i.e. tons of women now associating with you because of the letters on your jacket). The temptations can be quite daunting.

I even recall a student candidly discussing a fraternity party that he had just attended. He mentioned that at the party, there were two rooms the guys could go into for sex. There was a woman in one room giving oral sex, and the woman in the other room was giving vaginal sex. Believe it or not, one of the guys in the fraternity had found the women hitch hiking, and told them that if they wanted to get a ride to their destination, they had to perform this service for the organization. I guess this gives a new definition to the terms "party favors" or "community service". I was clearly shocked as he told me this story, which sounded alot like illegal activity.

This kid in the fraternity was a good student, with a relatively high grade point average. You would never have thought, based upon his grades, and the kind of family he came from, that he would participate in such a dastardly activity. But the peer pressure was incredibly strong, and he did find himself in the room with one of the women (which I guess he never told his girlfriend).

I don't tell this story to make fun of anyone, I tell it because these are the kinds of things that can happen on college campuses. Your babies are no longer babies. They are adults with entirely too much time on their hands, not enough maturity and lots of physical energy. As a result, you are going to have a lot of things happen on college campuses that do not happen in even the worst parts of society. It can be a frightening thing.

The emotional roller coasters

College is a time when many students are just starting to learn to deal with and manage their emotions. They are going through things that they've never experienced: love relationships, isolation from family, tough growth experiences, and loneliness. Depending on the psychological make up of the individual, how the student responds to their new environment is going to differ from one student to the next. Some students come to campus and are psychologically well adjusted and know how to deal with setbacks as they occur. There are other students who come to college and become emotional wrecks from the minute they arrive.

Most universities have counseling centers and other resources available to deal with students enduring emotional crises. Also, the resident advisors are taught to look out for students who may be going through some psychological hurdle.

During college, I had a roommate, let's call him Bill. Bill had never been away from home before, and being away from his family took a serious psychological toll out on him. The only thing Bill would do every day was lie in bed and watch television, only to leave occasionally for class. After class, he would camp out in front of the TV again. Bill was from a small town and had never been to "the big city", so he felt socially isolated in his new environment. I recall seeing Bill's dad packing his things into the trunk of the car. Bill said goodbye to me, and I never saw him again.

While many students adjust psychologically to college, it is much more common that the student is going to go through some temporary emotional crises. Yes, these usually have to do with the opposite sex. I can recall being dumped by the girl that I dated in college. Oh the heartbreak! My GPA fell through the floor that semester, as I spent all my time figuring out how to get this silly girl back. Years later, I have no idea why I liked this woman in the first place, since she wasn't all that pretty anyway.

Another temporary emotional crisis can occur if the student goes through a pregnancy scare or has a change in social status (up or down). For example, if the student joins a fraternity or sorority, they are suddenly bombarded with hoards of new "friends" that take up their time and make them think that they are something special all of a sudden. Of course, months later, half of these new friends have become enemies, but that is for them to learn and for us to know.

Pregnancy scares are something that many college students go through. Their parents usually have no clue when these scares occur. I have seen many a college female make that emergency trip with her best friend to the abortion clinic. I have nothing judgmental to say about this, other than to say that it happens. But having children is a natural thing, and sometimes it happens in college. Unfortunately, it can sometimes represent the end of the road for students attempting to pursue an education. Of course that is not always the case. My mother gave birth to me when she was in high school. She and my father were married at the age of 22, and they went on to finish college near the age of 30. Staying focused can help dreams come true.

Later in the book, I will talk about ways you and your child can prepare for these emotional crises. I am also going to talk about things you can discuss with them to make sure that even if you are not involved, they are going to be able to fight through the struggles and find their way to graduation.

The Frustrated
Parent

"I've spent $120,000 during the past 4 years, only to have my daughter get horrible grades and come home pregnant." – anonymous frustrated father of a college student.

During my years on a college campus, I have seen quite a few things. I have seen students live their dreams, and I have seen students create their nightmares from scratch. I have seen both students and parents do things that simply did not make much sense to me. Of course, I would never tell a parent or student what to do with their lives. I only share information, and biased information at that. The information is biased in the fact that it comes from my years of experience, and no one else.

I recall many years ago, watching an episode of "The Cosby Show". A group of mothers were sitting together, discussing their children's habits, and their achievements. At one point, Felicia Rashad (Claire Huxtable) says to the group "Does anyone have children doing AMAZING and WONDERFULE things with their lives?" Everyone in the group remained deathly silent, as their children had given them nothing to contribute. Then, Claire says something like "Does anyone have children who are lazy and driving them crazy?" With this call, the entire group perked up and every woman raised her hand, ready to contribute whatever terrible thing her child had recently done.

While much of this dialogue is reflective of what the typical parent goes through with their child, I admit that I found myself a bit confused by this conversation. The problems mentioned by these women simply did not go on in my house when I was a kid. Don't get me wrong, I was no prize for my parents. But I also knew that they didn't take any crap from me, and if I tried to dish them crap, I was going to have the crap put back in my face. My parents were just selfish enough to say that it was not the inborn right of their children to drive them to the insane asylum or the poor house, they also loved us enough to create a disciplined environment from the start. Some things that went on in other households were simply not going to happen in their home. So, you can imagine my confusion, as I watched this group of parents complain that their children were running their households. Such was not the luxury of my upbringing.

One of the things I've seen through the years is the prototypical "Frustrated Parent". This is the parent that comes to me and says: "I am bankrupting myself paying for my child to go to college, and he is bringing home terrible grades. He is not taking his education seriously, and I feel frustrated that I can't do anything about it."

I don't tell the parent what they should do. I do, however, share what I know about the environment. I tell them that basically, while many parents think that paying every single expense for their child is clearing time for the child to study more, it usually only gives the child a license to start their party weekend on Wednesday nights instead of waiting until Thursday. Additionally, I mention the idea that when I was the age of their son or daughter, tough love actually worked for me, and I question whether it is fair that the parent be the one to deal with the frustrations of this disagreement.

One of my best friends is a Professor of Psychology. During graduate school, he, like every other psychologist on this earth, was expected to train rats to run through mazes. I am not sure how they did it, but I am sure there was a method to the madness. Of course, this was a process that was full of trial and error. Sometimes the rat did what you needed it to do, sometimes it did not. But one of the things I've heard my friend say many times was that "There is no such thing as a dumb rat, there is only a dumb experimenter". What he was saying was that when the rat didn't do what you trained it to do, it might be tempting to blame the rat, but it might be necessary to analyze your training methods to determine if you've provided the right incentives. Was there enough cheese or too much? Did you teach the process incrementally, rather than all at once? (or perhaps more gruesomely) Did you put enough volts in the electric shock to let the rat know that he was going in the wrong direction?

As harsh as it may sound, humans, like rats, are trained through processes of reward and punishment created in our society. Most of us would not kill our enemies, because we know that we are going to go to prison for a very long time. We go to work every day because we know that if we do not, we are going to starve. If there were nothing forcing you to go to work every day and you had ten million dollars in the bank, would you go to work at your current job 5 days a week? If the answer is "yes", then congratulations. But if you are like many of us, the answer might be a resounding "No".

Children, in some ways, can be described as the rats that we are trying to train to run through the maze of life. That is part of your job as a parent, of which I am sure you are fully aware. One question that has to be asked all the time is "Are you creating the right incentives?" When a child makes a mistake or does something that simply does not make sense, we all have to ask ourselves if there was some incentive we did or did not create that would have changed the outcome.

What I see many times is that some students behave like damn fools on campus, and their parents do ABSOLUTELY NOTHING ABOUT IT. They complain, get angry, cuss, yell and scream, but they do nothing. I have never understood this. If we do not give our children the incentive to work hard and make the right decisions, I am not sure how we can expect them to work hard. Sure, working hard is the right thing to do, but many of us don't do the right thing because it is morally correct. Instead, we do the right thing because there is punishment for not doing so, and/or reward for doing what we are supposed to do.

I recall a student I had many years ago. He was a rich kid from Louisiana. He was on the swim team and seemed to think that "Partying" was his major, rather than Computer Science. He did not have to work, since his father sent him a check for several hundred dollars every month. He did not take his academics seriously, for he would simply tell me that he was going to take over his dad's business after graduation. But his father very badly wanted his son to perform well in class. So, to entice him to perform well, he told his son that if he earned a 3.5 Grade Point Average (on a 4.0 scale), he would buy him a $30,000 car. Now, this was during the early 1990s, so you can imagine how valuable such a car was back then ($30,000 will buy a nice car now!). You would expect a child to jump at this opportunity, get the excellent GPA, and show up on his dad's porch demanding delivery of his new vehicle. NOPE. The kid still plodded along with a horrific grade point average, never collecting on the new car, but eventually taking over his dad's business, which he ran into the ground.

There are several potential ways to handle the situation that I just described to you. Some might involve additional punishment for poor performance, but few would likely involve extra reward. But what was more interesting was that the parent may have been pushing the wrong buttons when it came to his son. As I look back on that experience, I ask myself some questions:

Why would the father want such a lazy, incompetent person running his company?

Does he not know that many fortunes have been squandered by incompetent offspring? I am sure that his father did not possess the same values as his son, since he was a successful businessman. So, it didn't make sense that he was willing to allow a lazy worker to run his firm just because the lazy bum was a relative.

Why was there no penalty for his son's behavior?

While his son was off at college getting into trouble, not studying very hard, I never once saw his father come in and punish his son for his behavior. The checks just kept coming, and the son seemed to feel that the parents posed no threat. It was almost as if he were the one controlling the situation entirely. Perhaps his son would have taken his education more seriously had his father stopped sending money. If getting more money was not a good motivator, then perhaps a lack of money would be a better way to get his son moving along.

Why did his father bear the entire brunt of every expense that his son incurred during college?

Was the son incapable of getting a job? In his defense, he was a collegiate athlete, which inhibited his ability to get a job during the season. However, he could have surely worked during the off-season and during the summer. Also, making his son work would have been symbolic in terms of making him "earn his keep". Since the son was not forced to use his spare time for anything productive, he did what many of us would have done, he squandered the time with meaningless, potentially destructive activities.

While I never met this student's parents, I am sure that they were frustrated by their son's lack of effort. But being next to him on a regular basis, I could see that his parents were simply not doing the necessary things to motivate him. So, in the end, when their son came home with mediocre grades and worked so hard to create a mediocre life, one can argue that they got exactly that for which they bargained.

Student Loans and Expenses – Can't the Child Do Anything?

"If you believe that any good American parent is supposed to pay for all of their adult child's expenses in college, I guess I must be a communist." – anonymous mother of a college student.

One of the most puzzling things in the world to me has been the obsession that many parents feel when it comes to their obligation to pay for their children's tuition, room board, books and all other expenses. Do they feel that their children are disabled? Do they not realize that their children are fully aware that their parents are doing things for them that they can do for themselves?

I recall hearing a student on her cell phone with her dad. She was pleading with her father to send money that she badly needed. She told him that she needed the money to pay for books, and that she couldn't find a way to get the money herself because her classes gave her too much work to do. I knew differently. She was a D- student in my class, so it was clear that she wasn't studying. After the conversation, she slammed her $700 cell phone shut and said to her friend "I can't go to the party. My dad wouldn't give me the money. He was like 'Get a job'. I can't believe he said that!" Knowing that her father was not going to give her the money, she went out and got a job. Had her father been easier on her, or listened to her sob story, she would have guilt-tripped him into believing that she could not work because she had soooo much studying to do. That is how things work on college campuses.

As you may already know, it is not easy to save for retirement. Current expenses eat up a great deal of the average American income, and it is difficult to put money aside in these circumstances. College is a tremendous expense. Many universities have tuition rates that exceed $30,000 per year, with the total costs approaching forty or fifty thousand. I am not sure how much money you have sitting around, but these numbers are enough to make a mummy wear a bathing suit to save money.

What is even more daunting is the fact that many parents that are sending their children to college are in the middle of the mad dash to save for retirement. So, tens and perhaps even hundreds of thousands of dollars that would have made for a much nicer retirement are being used to purchase a 4-year party for another healthy, capable, adult. Of course, the student himself/herself may not know that they are capable. I mean, after all, would you know that you could walk if you have been in a wheel chair your entire life? In fact, you probably would not be able to walk, since your muscles will have never grown strong enough to carry your own weight. If someone is always willing to push you around in the chair, you are going to always think that there is no alternative.

I will give you an example of the long-run financial impact of paying for your child to go to college. Let's assume that Bob and Mary have scrapped and saved for 10 years to put together a $120,000 nest egg for their child to attend college. That would be $30,000 per year x 4 years, which could be considered a conservative estimate, given that more and more students are taking 5 or even 6 years to finish college. After all, why not extend the party if it's on someone else's dime!

This couple is going to spend the $120,000 over the next 4 years, and the return on their investment *might* be that their child gets a college degree. During their child's years in college, she goes to campus, doesn't work and earns a mediocre grade point average. She goes on in life without student loans, and hopefully with a degree in hand. She *could* have gotten loans or a scholarship, but there was no point in doing so, since she already had someone willing to pay.

So, let's assume that instead of spending this money on college tuition, Bob and Mary save their $120,000 for retirement. They invest the money in a safe portfolio of treasury bills, earning 4.5% per year. This is a highly conservative investment, not nearly what they would earn investing in a diversified stock portfolio of average risk. Let's also assume that they are 40 years old, with 25 years left to retirement. How much additional retirement money would they have if they were to use the money for something else?

They would have a lot. Basically, at the rates I've given above, Bob and Mary would have an extra $360,652 to hang out at the beach. If they did this for 3 kids, they would have over $1 million. Additionally, if they were to invest the money for these 3 children at the historical growth rate of the stock market (12%), the number would be roughly $3.5 million.

Let's now assume that Bob and Mary have not been all that diligent in saving for their 3 children to go to college. So, because they have not saved through the years, they feel compelled to get loans to pay for the college education of their 3 children. They borrow the $360,000 necessary to send their 3 children to college at a loan rate of 5%. Given that this amount is large enough to be the mortgage on a very nice home, they stretch the loan terms out as far as they can. The payments are roughly $2200 per month, and they *end up making these payments until they are 70 years old.* What level of guilt does a parent have to feel to do such a thing, knowing that their children could have easily contributed the process?

Let's assume that Bob and Mary take a more constructive approach. First of all, rather than sending their children to a school that costs $30,000 per year, they send them to a university that only costs a total of $10,000 per year. A common fallacy is that spending more buys a better education. A lot of universities want you to believe that. But what is more important is how well you do when you go to college, not necessarily where you received your education. I went to a state university, and because I did so well while I was there, I beat out many Ivy League graduates for spots in top graduate programs.

I recall meeting a woman in a train station in Boston. The woman had gone to a very expensive private school. During our conversation, I realized that she was extremely bitter. After spending over $100,000 on her college education, she had an annual salary of about $25,000 per year, with a pile of student loans. If she could have done it over again, she would have gone to a state school. What made things even worse was that I had never heard of the school that she attended. For $100,000, you would at least expect that the school would have name recognition. Without that name recognition, potential employers are likely to think that you went to technical school or a junior college.

So, in the smart version of the story I mentioned above, Bob and Mary spend $10,000 per year on their children's educations, forcing each of them to contribute to the process by getting a job, applying for scholarships and taking on student loans themselves. The outcome is that rather than giving up $2.5 million in retirement funds, they are only giving up $800,000. They get to save $1.7 million in additional funds. And if they both live to the age of 82, this affords them an extra $100,000 per year to live, which is highly conservative, since I am assuming that they do not invest after the age of 65. In reality, the number would be substantially higher if the funds are invested in risk-free assets during the course of their retirement.

If you go farther and assume that Bob and Mary let their children find a way to fund their own college education, they save even more. If the children are sufficiently apart in age, another strategy might be to cover most of the expenses for the first child, and then allow that child to repay their loan from the family by becoming an active participant in contributing to the college expenses of the children that come after them. I have seen this strategy used in many families, and it seems to work.

There are a plethora of options that parents can take that won't put them in the poor house. Many college students are like the rest of us: whether they get the money from a job, a scholarship or their parents, it usually doesn't matter. All that matters is that they get the money from *somewhere*. The fact is that the parent should not feel guilty for taking away some of the party time and forcing the child to do something productive to earn their keep. The fact is that many students have parents who take on all their student loans, even though the child eventually gets a job making more money than their parents! Does this make sense to you?

What can happen when a student has no sense of purpose?

"I am going to stay in school an extra year so that I can pledge the sorority first." – anonymous student, when asked if she was planning to graduate from her $30,000 per year university the following semester.

Many of the students who struggle in college for social or academic reasons tend to be those who have no sense of purpose. If you ask them why they are in college, the answer might be something like "Because my dad said that I should do it." What do you think happens when someone is doing something they don't want to do, and they are doing it for someone else? They are going to be the biggest waste of money since the Federal Government. The student doesn't see the financial struggles of the parents that have afforded them a nice lifestyle. This is most true at universities in which the tuition cost is the highest. What is also true is the old saying: "An idol mind is a devil's workshop". The student with no sense of purpose with nothing but time on his/her hands is going to find things to do to utilize that time. They don't care if the outlet is productive or not. They only care that it takes their mind away from the miserable life that their parents have forced them to live.

How can parents combat this problem? First, the parent should make sure that the child plays some role in their collegiate choices. I do not recommend choosing your child's major for them, or playing too much of a role. Instead, you may want to give your child options with parameters. For example, if your child wants to major in something that is going to make it difficult to get a job, don't force them to major in Accounting or something that they are going to hate. You may want to let them choose a set of majors, allowing you to make the final recommendation from the set that they've chosen. You can also give them a set of options from which they can choose.

You can also force the child to shadow (follow around for a day) someone in their field, so that they can see what their life would be like if they choose that particular major. You may also want to compromise with the child. Allow them to minor in the area they like the most, with the agreement that they are going to major in something that will help them get a job later. The point is that the child has to be involved in the process. If they do not feel involved, they are going to get to college and be mentally lost. A student that is mentally lost is not likely to be able to appreciate the value of a college education.

Another potential problem is that because we shelter our children from the tough economic choices we must make, they do not always understand the value of a dollar or how hard it is to get the things that we buy for them. That can lead to the child simply wasting the parent's money. I recall taking my daughter to the store when she was 12. This time however, the birthday shopping trip was a little different. Rather than allowing her to choose a few things she wanted and my paying for them, I simply gave her a sum of money and let her make the purchase decision on her own.

To get this money in her hand was quite a thrill. She had never seen that much cash in real life before, so she thought she was Mrs. Rockefeller. However, when it came time to part with the cash during the shopping spree, you could see that her purchasing decision process had changed dramatically. Rather than looking at a rack and saying "I want that and that and that and that...", she would see things she wanted, but analyze them to decide which thing she wanted the most. She was doing things I had never seen her do before, like studying prices and comparison shopping. She would get things off the shelf, hold them for 20 minutes, and then reluctantly put them back. In fact, after the trip was over, she went home with half the money still in her pocket!

Of course, the moral of my daughter's story is quite simple: when kids are made responsible for their financial choices, they value them a great deal more. So, the obvious question is: why do parents not work harder to make the child feel the brunt of their financial struggles when their kids head off to college? Like my daughter BEFORE our informative shopping trip, the child comes to college with no idea of exactly how hard it is to pay $30,000 per year. So, when they are in college, it is difficult for them to understand the seriousness of what they are doing. It also becomes unnatural for them to take on the sense of urgency that we ourselves would have if we had paid this much to go to school.

The most important thing about helping your child feel a sense of purpose in college is to find ways to make them feel that they are captains of their own destiny. Let them feel and understand that they are not only involved in key decisions, but they are also responsible for key mistakes made in the process. Feeling such a strong sense of connection to the process and its outcomes are the keys to having a purposeful connection to your destiny.

Ways the Parent can Combat the Cramming Problem

"I feel so bad for my child. He studies 10 hours a day, and he still failed 4 of his classes" – anonymous parent, who didn't realize that her child was a complete liar.

Believe it or not, there are ways that parents can fight the tendency for their children to cram and engage in inconsistent studying while on campus. The role of the parent should not be that of one who simply stands frustrated that the child won't do what they are supposed to do. The reality is, that to some extent, you have a tremendous ability to impact the choices of the child on campus, and to help the child at least make sure they don't waste your hard earned money.

One of the most, if not the most, valuable lessons I learned during college had to do with cramming. I have never been a person that enjoyed missing sleep. I loved my sleep like I loved my own mother. It was my time to recharge my batteries and access things in my dreams that I had not yet obtained in real life. A long, difficult day was much easier to deal with when I'd had plenty of sleep than it was when I'd had very little.

In fact, I would say that sleep was my best friend. There would be those days when I would get out of bed, say on a rainy day. I might be groggy from not sleeping well the night before, so I might not even go to class under normal circumstances. The difference on this day is that I have a very important quiz, perhaps one for which I am not fully prepared.

On the way to class, I am already feeling emotionally heavy from the damp, dreary day that lies before me. It is chilly outside, and I didn't even wear a thick enough jacket. After waking up 20 minutes too late, I was forced to run out the door without taking a shower. So, not only am I filthy and stinking, I am also feeling emotionally filthy due to the nasty weather. Ever have one of those days when you wake up and you ALREADY KNOW that it's raining because the air is so thick? It's one of those days.

On the way to class, I step in a muddle puddle, and I am drenched, since I forgot to bring my umbrella. As I damply walk into class, I glance quickly toward my spot in the room so that I can sit down and begin my quiz. But there is no one in the room. In a panic, I sprint across campus (taking another 15 minutes that I don't have, since I was already 10 minutes late) to the office of the departmental secretary to find out where the quiz was being held. Apparently, when I missed class the other day, my professor had changed the location of the quiz. Some professors do this when they feel that the room is not going to be big enough to fit all of their students at one time. You see, on most days, only 90% of all students show up to class. But quiz and exam days are the only times that 100% of the students are in class.

I find the number of the room in which the exam is being taken, which is of course all the way across campus. So, another rain-drenched 15 minutes later, I am finally walking into the correct classroom. My teacher, an older guy with a scary gray beard and little glasses that hang off his nose, peers at me over his glasses as if to say "Where have you beeeeeeeen young man?" I try to explain, but the words don't come out. I just take my quiz and sit down.

Of course, when it rains it pours. The quiz is an absolute monster! The biggest nightmares are when you dream that you are having a nightmare. I flunk the quiz with flying colors, particularly since I only have 20 minutes to finish a 1-hour assignment. To make things even worse, I find out later that because the quiz was so difficult, the teacher had given the entire class a tremendous and helpful set of hints to help them get through the quiz. Of course, these hints are erased from the board by the time I arrive. This is a classic day from hell that every college student goes through at least once.

On days like this, sleep is my salvation. Afterward, I would not go to my next couple of classes (yes, this choice is bad, but this is an emergency!). Instead, I head to my dorm and sleep like a baby with a stomach full of mashed carrots. I sleep like I am never going to wake up again. After waking up 4 hours later, I restart my day and find that the sun is now shining, I can go visit my professor and smooth things over, and my life is sort of back on track. Not quite, but at least I am now able to smile.

This describes how important sleep is to me, and how it mattered most to me in college. After gaining such an attachment to sleep, you can see how necessity became the mother of my invention. I would see students heading to class on exam day, looking like zombies on Viagra. I would see them going to class with their hair turned in every direction, and the eyeballs of heroin addicts. All of this deprivation simply the result of staying awake for the previous 3 nights, and living off a steady diet of coffee, no-doze and any other Performance Enhancing Academic Steroid they can find, some of them legal, some of them not.

Cramming can be physically and mentally unhealthy to say the least. I have seen many students end up in psychotherapy after dealing with the stress of cramming. Ulcers are a natural artifact of this kind of behavior, and it's an easy way to get absolutely nothing for your efforts. I cannot tell you how many times I've had students come into my office and say "I studied for the test all night, but I still failed." Well, that is usually what happens when you try to learn a month's worth of material in one day!

The silly thing about cramming is that this is yet another stupid American college tradition. I am not sure who spread the lie that cramming is what you do in college, because I need to talk to that person and whack him in the head. If you want to get minimal results for maximum effort, then you should cram. If you want to drive yourself insane, then you should cram. If you want to miss sleep and end up depressed all the time, you should cram. If you want to hate college, you should cram. Cramming is the way to make all your anti-dreams come true.

I never wanted to be a zombie. I loved my sleep too much. So, rather than being another brain-drenched crammer, I found a better solution to cramming, sort of an alter ego. I called it "Jamming". This was, I think, the beginning of my awareness of how silly people can be, and ways that I can keep myself from being equally stupid.

To explain Jamming, I should first say that it is really no different from cramming. If you want to stay up all night, you can. If you want to use Performance Enhancing Academic Steroids (the coffee and no-doze), you can. If you want to be a zombie, then there are ways to do this. But the healthy approach can be one where you simply work consistently hard, and with a strong, firm sense of urgency.

The major difference between "Jamming" and it's evil brother "Cramming" is TIMING. Cramming occurs right before the next exam, Jamming occurs right AFTER the previous one. The key principal that defines the difference between the two approaches is this: Whether you Jam or Cram, you are going to have to learn all the material anyway. It's like paying an old bill. If you pay it a year late, your credit is going to be destroyed. But if you pay it on time, you will get an excellent credit rating. But either way you slice it, the dues have to be paid.

When I engaged in Jamming, I basically used the emotion built up from the last test. If I did poorly, I would walk out of the exam saying to myself "This stuff is never going to happen again!" Have you ever had a day like that, where you were humiliated, and swore that you were not going to let the disappointment happen again? But later, the emotion wears off, and history ends up repeating itself? What about all those passionate New Years resolutions? If you are like the rest of us, you rarely have a resolution that makes it past Easter.

Well, what happens to all this passionate energy? Why not bottle it up and find a way to use it while it's good and hot? That is what Jamming is all about. They key to Jamming is that you are using your emotional state to propel you to work hard in the future. The other nice thing is that whether you performed poorly on the last test or had a strong performance, you always have a reason to feel inspired. If I did really well on a test, I would say to myself "Wow, I'm pumped! I am going to kick even more butt on the next test." The key is that you use this energy positively, no matter where the emotion is derived.

So, over the next week, I would study like my life depended on it. If the next test was going to cover 5 chapters, I would read all five during the first week. If each chapter takes 1.5 hours to read, I could have them all read in a day or two. For some reason, students think that it takes forever to read a bunch of chapters at once, but they are always able to do it when the exam is the following day. If I had time, I would read the chapters more than once. I would also go through any slides or lecture notes that the professor was going to go over during the following month, as I made it my personal quest to know more about the topic than the professor did.

Here are the benefits of Jamming:

1) You can get a lot more bang for your studying buck. As a professor, one of the things that I do is ask simple questions from the chapter that students are told to read in order to prepare for class. Most students do not read the chapter before the class. Instead, they usually wait until after the class or right before the exam to read it. In fact, out of 50 students who are told to read the chapter before the class, less than 3 or 4 usually do it. The student(s) who have read the chapter in advance are the ones that I am going to remember the most, even if they are not good students. What is so sad about this is that EVERYONE IN THE ROOM is going to read the chapter at some point. So, the ones who have read the material early are going to get more credit for their work. These perceptions can go a long way, since the students who are able to answer my small questions before everyone else are going to be the ones identified as being the best in my class.

2) The Jamming student is relaxed the week of the exam. The cramming student is one Scooby snack away from the insane asylum. This is not the way to live in college. Cramming can be what makes some students hate college, while other students love it. In fact, I would say that the students who love college are in one of two categories: either they jam/study consistently and make good grades or they are lazy and pathetic and make bad grades. I say this because the students who make bad grades are not worried as much about the grades they get,

so they are not stressed about it. They just accept whatever C or D lands on their doorstep, and they then turn around and finish partying. The students who tend to hate college the most are the A and B students who cram. The common denominator is STRESS. Few of us enjoy being under constant stress and pressure. The students who do well in college via cramming are the ones that are always in poor health, overwhelmed and nervous. They are the ones dying to get out of school because they end up hating it so much. While there are exceptions, stress can be the defining factor differentiating those students who are happy and those who are not.

3) One of the things I like to do in my class is give pop quizzes to students in order to determine which ones have read the chapters in advance and which ones have not. These quizzes are designed to reward those students who Jam and don't Cram. Also, it is designed to give struggling students a chance to mend their grades, since the quizzes are set up so that they can only improve student grades, not hurt them. Here is what I do: I find 5 really easy questions from the following chapter, and I ask them on the quiz. The student that has already read the chapter is going to get 5 free points, while the smart student who likes to cram is going to be irritated, since they are going to learn the very same material later that day when I teach it during class.

4) When I ran track in high school, I found out that getting ahead early in the race was always a good way to win, especially in sprints. When you are in front, the pressure is on the other runners to catch you, and you just have to keep doing what you are

doing. College is the same way. If you are on top of the game, things are much easier. By maintaining the momentum you have created, you can go on to win the race with flying colors. The students who jam are the ones working from ahead, so they find themselves in front at the finish line also.

5) Jamming students have a MUCH better understanding of the material. Think of things that you know very well that you learned years ago, perhaps a skill. Let's assume that someone wants to spend the same number of hours learning the skill that you have, but they are going to condense all these hours in one year. Would they have mastered the skill as well as you have? No. This person is still not going to know their stuff as well as you because you've had time to let it sink in, while they have not. Jamming students get to see the material 3 times: before class, during class and after class/before the exam. Each time they see the stuff, they are going to understand it volumes better than they did before. Cramming students are going to be confused during class, and they are also not going to learn it very well when they cram later, since there is so much to learn all at once. So, the sooner your child learns the lessons of Jamming, the better off they are going to be.

6) Most professors grade on serious curves, so if the other students are still slow and groggy from the summer, Jamming gives your child a chance to dominate the class. Basically, class averages on exams are typically much lower right after the summer than they are during the rest of the year. This is because students are coming back from

vacation and their brains are "not in shape" from their time off. So, sitting and studying for 5 hours is a lot more difficult early in the year than it is later, when there is a sense of urgency and the students have gotten into the swing of things. A sharp student can take advantage of the weakness of their peers by basically attacking the game early and getting their study skills together before the other students are ready to go.

How to Make your Child Prepared for College

"I gave my mother my applications and she didn't send them. I also asked for her tax information, and she refused to give it to me." – anonymous student- angry at her mother for not being cooperative as she tried to prepare for college.

Before we even begin a discussion on how to best prepare your child for college, I should start by saying that preparation can be over-rated. The students who do well/best in college are not those that are best prepared, but rather, those who are ready to do their best at all times. If I could choose between two students, a lazy student with a perfect SAT score and an incredibly hard working student with an SAT score far below average, I would choose the second student IN A HOT SECOND. The reason is that one of the most significant myths of college is that there are some students who are genetically designed and prepared for college and those who are not. If this pre-destination had any merit, then it would not be the case that there are a disproportionate number of minority students in special education. Lack of intellect knows no racial boundaries, so it is likely the bias of the educational system and our social systems that lead us to think that one child is inherently better than another.

We should also discuss the fact that it is *flat out stupid* to tell someone at the age of 18 what they are capable of doing for the rest of their lives. Think about how much you've changed since the age of 18. I don't know about you, but in many ways, I am not even the same person. There were stupid things I would have done back then that I would not even think of doing right now. Imagine the mental differences between age 18 and 45? What about 18 and 55? Well, given that we know how much someone changes after the age of 18, *why in the world* do we force them to make choices that will throw away the lives they are going to be forced to live when they are in their 40s, 50s and 60s? If a counselor tells some gum-smacking teenager that he is not meant to go to college, then that counselor is promoting the idea that this child, because of what they've done during their youth, should be stricken to a life of educational, financial, social and personal mediocrity. They are saying that, even 20 years later, this person will not have obtained the tools necessary to be a college graduate. At the same time, the counselor turns toward other students from wealthier families or better grades and tells them that this life is open to them. That is like admitting some people to an eternity of heaven and rejecting others, all based on the shape of their ears.

A College Preparatory Curriculum

In addition to the things I've just mentioned, I should tell you that if you can, it is best to make sure that your child has taken courses that will make college easier for him/her. Having taken these classes does not guarantee success, since the classes are usually easier than what we give in college. But they do push the child to a higher level of understanding than the other students around them. Not taking these classes does not, however, exclude the student from being able to go to college and do well. It just makes it a little tougher.

If you are not sure what your child should be taking to get ready for college, ask your high school if they have a curriculum designed to prepare students for college. If they do not, then try calling or checking on the Internet at a local university to find out what students need to have taken before they come to campus. All of this information is going to be very helpful, and you can get it all by making just a couple of phone calls.

You may want to do what you can to encourage your child to work hard in these courses, although I know this is difficult. But perhaps you can simply set some boundaries: 3 hours with the TV off working on homework, with 5-minute breaks given every 45 minutes. You can also encourage the child to study in the library, where it is quiet and relaxing. Give them a chance to get a nap before they begin work, and then let them have breaks so that the studying does not get monotonous.

Help your child get mentally prepared for college

Your child also needs to go through a process in which you help them translate from a high school mentality, to one that is going to make them successful in college. This has always baffled me, but I have heard of many high schools that don't give any homework. What? Not that I am a believer in homework, I have always hated it as much as the next person. But the idea that the school doesn't give the students anything to do at home is simply absurd.

To combat some of these issues, you should find homework for your child. It doesn't have to be anything difficult, just reading assignments and things that require the student to write. Practice in writing and reading are critical for college. When I was a student in high school, I failed English many times. However, I eventually learned what a good sentence looked like by reading a lot. I learned to write by keeping a journal for several years when I was in college. I would write down my thoughts, and although I stopped keeping the journal after a few years, I gained a great deal during the time it was in existence. By doing some of these things, your child can be in a position to do what is basically expected in college: reading and writing.

Another aspect of preparing your child mentally for college is to have him/her read a book that tells them about college and what to expect. For example, in my book *Everything you ever wanted to know about college*, I talk about all the things that happen in college outside the classroom, as well as what happens inside it. These issues are critical, since your child must be prepared to make the right decisions. These readings should be supplemented by conversations with your child about college and the life choices they are going to have to make when they are there.

You may also try to let them have a conversation with someone that is already in college or someone who has already attended. Don't just let them talk to one person, since that is going to give them a biased perspective. Have them talk to multiple people if you can. If you don't know anyone who has gone to college, take them to a local campus and have them meet with a random student that happens to be walking by. I am sure the student will be happy to talk to your child and if not, the next student probably will.

You may want to also have your child take a college course or two during high school, or at least during the summer after high school graduation. This can give them a first hand account of what college is going to be like. Choose something easy, not a killer course that will intimidate them later. Some universities may not allow easy enrollment of high school students, but many of them are happy to take your money. Also, your child doesn't have to have perfect grades to take intro college classes, they only have to show up ready to work hard.

Many universities have pre-college summer programs designed to prepare students for college. These programs may have restrictions that are based on the race, family income or ACT score of the student. But you should check to find out if your child qualifies for any of these programs. Many of them are very good, since they give the child the chance to come onto campus and experience college life first hand, before the other students arrive on campus. These programs are designed to basically give the student a chance to go through some growing pains early and level the playing field relative to those students who might have already had some college experience. I highly recommend these programs if you can find them. If there is no such program, then sending your child to take classes in the summer is the next best thing.

Remedial courses during the summer can be a wonderful way to get your child up to speed on topics that the child may find difficult. Many state universities and community colleges have courses that could be taken by an ambitious elementary school student. I mention this to say that no matter what kind of deficiency your child may have, there is always a way to overcome it, with a step-by-step process.

Let's assume that your child only does math on a second grade level. That child could take a very basic arithmetic class from a local community college, then take the next class, say in Pre-Algebra. If the child does well in those two courses, they can then move on to College Algebra, the class taken by many university freshmen throughout the country. This catch-up process can take place in as little as one summer or a year. It is not hard to learn what we teach you in college, the bricks in the walls around you are not required for you to learn. If a person is ambitious and wants to learn, they can learn as much between the ages of 18 and 20 as most people learn in a lifetime.

Building a Child who Studies Consistently

"My child studied very consistently in college, even though his grades did not seem to show it. But it was not until later that I realized he does all of his studying in front of the TV." – anonymous parent.

I have to say that in my experience, the best-kept secret of college success comes in the form of consistency. It's very simple: the students that know how to study consistently strongly outperform those that do not. The students that end up getting clobbered by the college experience are the ones that let everything pile up. These are also the students who walk away from college thinking that it is incredibly difficult, while those who study consistently end up saying "It wasn't all that bad." Many of the greatest problems that plague all of us have very simple solutions. This is no exception. A student that knows how to simply sit down and study every day for just a few hours is going to be light years ahead of those who do not.

The analogies to help us see this clearly are far too abundant to mention. If I start off walking 2 miles per hour one month before you, and I walk for 10 hours per day, I am going to cover about 600 miles. That is the distance between New York and Kentucky. That means that if you try to make that same trip at the last minute in a Porsche, or even on a jet airplane, I am going to get there before you. What is even more telling about this scenario is that the cost of chartering a jet or renting a Porsche is astronomical compared to the cost of using your feet. The same analogy would apply even more strongly if I were driving a slow car. If I drive 30 miles per hour and leave one week ahead of you, I am going to have a nice, relaxing drive and get there far ahead of you, no matter how fast you drive at the end.

The foolhardy student is the one that thinks "If I drive fast enough, my Porsche can catch up with your bicycle." That is not true if you are leaving 3 weeks later than the person riding the bike. So, this leads to those students who study extremely hard the two days before the exam, driving their Porsches until the wheels fall off, to be consistently defeated by those students who casually ride their bikes every day after school.

Cramming is the counterpart to not studying consistently. Jamming is one way to combat the lack of consistency, but it is not the only solution, nor is it the most effective. Additionally, it is not a catchall to solving the problem of student inconsistency.

Why it is tough to be consistent

Part of the consistency problem is very simple. It comes down to the absence of immediate feedback and gratification. Like the dog of the famous psychologist Pavlov, many of us are unable to force ourselves to do work that we need to do if there is no immediate reason to do it. Most of us have gone through the frustration of backing ourselves into a corner, swearing that we will NEVER let this happen again, only finding ourselves in the same predicament time after time.

College students are the worst when it comes to committing some of the personal sins that plague us all. What is most costly about this weakness is that it occurs during a time when we are making some of the most important decisions in our lives. What we do in college pays off 10 fold in the future, while putting in that same amount of effort at the age of 35 does not help us nearly as much. The student that realizes this early is the one that is going to get ahead, plain and simple. It was when I figured out how to "Jam" and to study consistently that I suddenly rose head and shoulders above my peers in college. For everyone else, finals week was full of stress. For me, it was vacation time.

Teach them to think of school like a job

One of the funniest things about human beings, especially college students is that while we have the ability to go to work 10 hours a day for $8 an hour, we don't have the ability or desire to study 5 hours a day to get much more. The difference is that a) the test is not for another month, so it doesn't seem urgent and b) the financial payoff is not immediate. That is one of the irrational components of human nature. Most of us would not pay 25% interest on a loan, but by giving up $1,000 in the future to get $100 now, we are paying far more than 25% interest.

Here is the logic I use with students to help them to understand the value of working consistently, as well as how to do it. I say "Look, you work at McDonalds and you have no problem doing 8 hours a day during the summer, right?" The student says "Yes". I then tell them "So, studying 4 hours a day is much easier, right? You don't have to stand on your feet, it's doesn't take as much time, and you get a much higher payoff in the future. Does it make sense to work that hard for McDonalds, but not that hard for yourself?"

While this does not always get the student motivated, it at least makes them fully aware that they are being inconsistent with the way that they are investing their time. As most of us know, awareness is the first step toward solving the problem. If you can at least get the student to understand that their current approach is suboptimal, they will begin to desire to do something different. At that point, you draw the map to help them at least set goals that are consistent with what they want to do. You have to be aware, however, that the ability to set a goal and then perform the day-to-day activities necessary to execute your strategy is a growth process that does not happen overnight. It is hit and miss, and full of frustration along the way. Be patient with your child as you watch them stumble along through this process.

You may want to also tell them that if they let a day go by without studying, they are probably not doing something right. Perhaps they can have one day off per week, but they should rarely take any day off completely. You can encourage the student to allocate some minimum number of hours every day to study, so that they stay on top of their courses.

One good thing to encourage your child to do is to go over the class notes right after the class in which they heard them. That way, the notes are fresh in their mind, and they can absorb the information much easier than if they were trying to learn it all at once.

The bottom line is that you should instill in your child very early the value of treating school as their first job. Studying is something that is to be done every day, not only on special occasions, such as exams and quizzes.

The "Eat your vegetables first" approach

The thing about studying every day is that it can also set you free. Once you've done your time for the day, you should be free to do what you want. As a student, I went through some periods when I didn't want to be in school anymore, let alone study. But because I knew the value of my education, I forced myself to continue. As a result, I would make deals with myself, like "Ok, I am going to put in (some minimal number) of hours every single day. If I don't want to do more, I am not going to. But if I want to stay longer, I will. Once my time is done, I am going to go to 3 parties and have a blast."

The idea behind this approach is that you are honest in terms of understanding that life is not just for working all the time. Sometimes, we want to relax. The key is to not let the relaxation go overboard. Things pile up very quickly, so you would be AMAZED at the difference between a little bit of work and none at all. It's a lot like gaining weight: a person that exercises 20 minutes per day for 3 days per week is going to look much different from someone that doesn't exercise at all. That is because the non-exercising person is going to let all the little bits of fat pile up and find themselves having to put butter on their hips to get through the door.

Explaining the value of study location to your child

If you call your child and ask them where they are studying, please don't let them tell you "I am in front of the TV." Studying in front of the TV is about an inch better than not studying at all. The student that really wants to learn what they need to know is not one that uses part of their brain to process a rap video in the background while trying to learn Biology at the same time.

When you talk to your child, explain to them that where they study is as important as how long they study.

Also, choosing the right place to study is a good way to develop the right kinds of habits. Students should go to a place that is quiet, away from distractions, with plenty of light. This forces the brain to engage in maximum concentration, helping the person to absorb as much information as possible. The brain works a lot like a computer: if there are a lot of things going on at once, it is not nearly as effective or efficient.

You should also encourage your child to take a pair of earplugs wherever they go, and a textbook. That way, when they are at work, or waiting in line, they can pull the book out and get some reading done. There is a lot of waiting in line during college, and if something goes wrong, you can end up wasting an entire day. It can be daunting and discouraging to spend the whole day waiting, only to find several hours of studying waiting for you when you get home.

Whatever you do, DO NOT ENCOURAGE YOUR CHILD TO STUDY IN THE DORM ROOM. Dorms are horrible places to study. Imagine trying to get work done with all your best friends coming to bang on your door every few minutes? You would be about as productive as a person that is asleep. Share these facts with your child, for in their youth, they may not know about these bad habits.

Help your child to hold him/herself accountable for their actions

One of the best ideas I came up with during college to help me study was when I started to find creative ways to make sure that I was staying on track with my goals. This is no different from the kind of feedback system that a company would use to track employee spending or to see if they are getting results. The funny thing about college students is that most of them are lazy. I hate saying it, but laziness is part of all of our psyches, and it usually takes a good kick in the butt to get it out of us. If you were to do a campus survey and ask students if they are lazy, about 10% of them would say "yes", while the rest of them would say "no". That is human nature and reminds us that as young people, we are not very good at taking responsibility for our actions.

What is also telling is that if you were to ask students how many hours they study on a typical day, many of them would say "About 4 or 5." I find this quite interesting, since many of these same students would have "C"s or "D"s in my class. I can't tell you how many students I've had come and tell me ridiculous things like how they studied for my test 12 hours a day for 3 weeks straight. I laugh inside, because I know that anyone who studies for my class that much is going to know the material better than I do.

Where is the disconnect here? Is it that students are lying to us? Sometimes. It can also be the case that they are lying to themselves. We all do that. I can't tell you how many times I would say that I run 1 mile every day, when it's really more like ½ mile every 4 days. But 1 mile per day is my goal, so that is what I think that I am doing. Students can do the same thing. When they say "I study 4 or 5 hours per day", what they are really trying to say is "I study 4 or 5 hours per day *on the days that I study* (which might be only 3 days per week), and this includes every single second that I spend in front of a book, not excluding time that I spend taking breaks, talking on the phone, going to the bathroom, or joking with my friends."

An important thing for students to understand is that there is a difference between study time and QUALITY study time. The contrast is no different from that of a Pepsi that is 100% pure, and another one that has two drops of Pepsi, mixed with a gallon of water. You can argue that both of them are sodas, but which is going to taste more like a Pepsi?

As a freshman in college, I began the long and trying quest of learning to be honest with myself. I noticed that many times, I was never working as hard as I claimed to or as hard as I thought I was. I noticed that on days when I was forced to study a subject I disliked, I would sit in front of the book for 4 hours, taking extra long bathroom breaks, reading magazines and doing anything OTHER than studying the subject at hand. In the end, I would stop and say to myself "Well, I did 4 hours of that stuff, so I'm done!"

I then decided to start using a technique that I still use to this day, even though I am no longer a student. I create what I call a "Study time sheet". This sheet was very simple, and it included a list of 3 columns on a sheet of paper: the time I started and stopped studying the subject, the total amount of time I spent on the topic, and the name of the topic itself. I would then set my goals based on the time sheet. For example, I would say "My goal for this week is to study a total of 50 hours." I would not include break time, bathroom time, or anything that had nothing to do with studying. So, there were times when I was forced to sit in front of the book for 8 hours in order to clear 6 hours of work. But the reality was that, in the end, I was being honest with myself, and I had a clearer, more direct connection between my efforts and my outcomes.

You may want to encourage your child to use this same approach. One of the added benefits of this approach were that, at the end of each day, I was holding myself accountable for *how much work I had done that day*. That way, no matter how well I was doing in the class, I had a direct, more immediate measure of my standing. If I was working extremely hard (i.e. putting in good hours every day), I knew that my grades were going to improve. If I was being a lazy-butt, I knew I was in for a rude awakening. This encouraged me to be more consistent with my work and my actions, sort of like how getting a paycheck at the end of the day is going to make you work more consistently than getting one at the end of the year.

The second benefit of this approach is that I was able to rely on one fundamental, important underlying principle that affects all mankind: you usually get what you pay for. That means that I no longer had to worry about what individual professors were thinking or doing in their courses. I just knew that if someone studies 5, 6, or 7 hours every single day of the week, they are usually going to get a good grade. Sometimes, I would get a "B" when I deserved an "A". Sometimes, it would be the other way around. Either way, I usually got what I earned, and that was a great feeling.

Eventually, I no longer set personal academic goals that depended on grades. I set goals based on EFFORT, which was something that I could control. Being able to control the thing that is most related to your goals helps you manage emotional distress, since you know that you and not someone else, are the one who ultimately decides your outcomes in life. Had I set my goals based on grades, I would have been stressed out over what grade this professor or that one was going to give me. That is a very powerful feeling. The more directly empowered your child can feel, the happier they are going to be.

Teach them the art of daily renewal

One of the other keys to consistency again relies on the idea of immediate feedback and gratification. This can come through a process of daily renewal and accountability.

Working hard toward your goals can be tough and emotionally draining. There are tough days when you wonder why it's even worth it to move forward, so you have to find a way to keep going, even when it seems that you have every reason not to do so. Therefore a person should learn healthy coping mechanisms to get through these stressful moments.

Many students manage stress through unhealthy coping mechanisms. They use alcohol and drugs, they engage in other pleasure-seeking activities, or they just might give up altogether. These are natural responses to the same stress that challenges us all.

First of all, you should make sure that your child clearly understands that the road to self-improvement is paved with stress and failure. That is just a simple fact of life. So, as they try to implement a new system of study, they are going to find themselves disappointed on a regular basis and at times, ending the day flat out exhausted.

This is where the system of self-renewal comes into play. It's basically a process where you end the day, taking an inventory of what you've done. You then evaluate yourself in a non-judgmental fashion and figure out how and why tomorrow is going to be different from the day before. What students will find is that many times, what seemed to be a daunting task yesterday is more manageable today. A good night's sleep can make all the difference in the world.

The other part of this process involves sitting and doing an inventory of your day before it even begins. You might start by saying to yourself "What do I want to try to get done today? What do I have on my calendar? How much time do I have for studying?" You ask those questions and then with a piece of paper, make an outline of how the day is going to go. Also, you try to figure out *what you are going to do on this day* to make your goals into a reality. Constantly refreshing and renewing yourself each day is not only a way to recharge your batteries, but it keeps the process toward self-improvement fresh and new.

Understanding where habits come from

If you want your child to create the good habits of a consistent studier, you have to spend some time thinking about the power of habits. Like everything else, a habit is one of the most powerful things in our world. Love is a habit. Drugs are a habit. Sex is a habit. Shopping, smoking, sleeping, and watching TV? All habits.

Most of us think of habits as a bad thing, and in many cases, they are. They control us and lead us to do things without even thinking about them. We are usually aware of our bad habits, and don't think much about our good ones and how they benefit us. Good habits, equally powerful, are autonomous ways for us to better our lives without even thinking about it.

The beautiful and sometimes frightening thing about the human subconscious is that it doesn't care one way or the other about whether or not our habit is good or bad, healthy or unhealthy, fulfilling or deadly. It only writes the habit down and makes sure that it is executed. These habits are created through repetition. The more we do something repeatedly, the more it becomes pre-programmed into our psyche.

I remember the funny dilemma I would go through when it came to studying. At the start of every semester, I HATED STUDYING. I would sit down for 20 minutes, and before long, I would be fidgeting like a 2 year old in a highchair trying to get to a toy truck on the floor. It was terrible! But knowing that I needed to keep working to make progress, I would force myself to work. I would give myself little breaks, lots of them. I would sometimes stop early, but I would get a little better every day. After about 2-3 weeks, I would be humming along like a well-oiled Mercedes, studying as much as 10 hours a day without breaking a sweat. I would be the envy of my friends, all of whom couldn't muster out an hour of studying on a good day.

The question is "How does a person who cannot sit for 20 minutes straight become someone that can work for 10 hours a day?" *It was the power of habit formation.* Basically, by forcing myself to sit in that seat for longer periods of time every day, my body and mind eventually accepted the fact that I was going to have to be there for a while. My butt would get more comfortable in the seat, and my brain would not tell me to leave until later and later in the day. I was *becoming addicted to studying!* I eventually would get to the point that *not studying* on a certain day would make me feel uneasy, as if I wasn't doing what I was supposed to do. I would keep my books with me and even if there were other things out there to do, I would want to put in my time.

I was no different from a typical drug addict. Sitting and working toward my goals created natural chemical flows in my brain that I eventually became addicted to. The feeling would have been no less strong had I been in love, or using drugs. The difference was that I was doing something positive. This is the typical case of a common workaholic.

Explain to your child the importance of forming good habits when they work everyday. Tell them that studying in the right place every day matters, since that is where they are going to be used to studying. Also, tell them that although it is extremely difficult at first, they should force themselves to go through the habit repetition necessary to become a strong studier. As a parent, explaining this part of human nature to them will help them understand themselves much better.

You may want to use a sports analogy. Studying every day is something that requires you to "get in shape". Tell them to expect difficulty at first, but once they get into shape "for the season", they are going to have an easier time "making it through practice". This can help if you have a child who once played sports. Most athletes understand the idea of doing something every day on the field to reach their long-term goals. You would only be helping them to redirect their energies into the right direction.

Combating Complacency

"It shouldn't be that difficult to earn a 4.0 in college, I did it in high school all the time."- anonymous in-coming freshman student who later dropped out after earning a 1.1 GPA during her freshman year.

Prototype of the complacent student

In my mind and my experience, there is a prototype of the complacent student. This is the one that is about to be whacked in the head by reality, and years later, they are giving speeches to other students on how they should not "do what I did". The student is usually someone that did very well in high school, perhaps they won some awards, maybe a giant scholarship. They usually have excellent grades and a top-notch ACT score. They may even be on their way to a top university, perhaps Harvard or Stanford, choosing some complicated major in which you have to have an IQ above 150 just to pronounce the name of the subject. This is a wonderful thing, and many of the students in this category go on to do wonderful things..............Then, of course, there are the students who do not. The bad version of these students end up in two categories: either they sink into mediocrity, perhaps either becoming C and B students, or they end up as complete disasters: become so emotionally traumatized and demoralized by their experience that they just give up all together.

I am quite saddened when I see this kind of thing happen. Many students come to college with a world of potential, only to allow one bad experience in a Calculus class or one tough semester to lead them down the path toward major mistakes. It's just the saddest thing in the world for me. Most successful people later realize that even if you are the most gifted in your field, the battle toward turning that gift into victories is going to be a tough one. Even Michael Jordan, the basketball player, had to bite and scratch for every championship he won. Had he expected them to come easily just because he was Michael

114

Jordan, he would have won nothing. Greatness is shown by reaching the goal, not by *having the potential* to reach it.

I will share some tips with you on ways to combat the risk of complacency for your child. This is a tough battle to fight, but if you fight it properly, you can propel your child forward through some tough experiences.

The freshman year is not the 13th grade

You are going to have let your child know loud and clear "College is NOT in any way shape or form, a simple continuation of high school." The child must understand fully that they are entering a different world all together, and the idea that they are going to be able to just waltz into college and dominate as they did in high school is going to lead them to have major problems later on. They should be made to understand that the road to high school success was very tough, in which they started from the bottom and worked their way up. They should be prepared to do the same thing in college.

The professors they encounter in college are not going to care, one way or the other, about whether or not they were top students in high school. We treat all students the same, whether they received the Presidential Scholarship or nothing at all. The new goal for all students is to reprove themselves to their new teachers, showing them that they are capable of doing well at the next level.

They should also know that since the terrain has changed, success strategies in one area do not necessarily breed success in another. So, students should not think that their "tried and true" success strategies in high school are going to work in college. The child needs to have an open mindset, one in which they are open to new approaches to studying with no commitment to old techniques that have been known to work. One of the most common mistakes of college students is using the same approach they used in high school. They find quickly that the ball game has changed.

Teach your child the values of a warrior

A child should understand when they get to college that it is the work ethic that drives success, nothing else. The child has to come to college with a preconceived notion of how they are going to deal with failure. Are they going to lie down and take it, or are they are going to try a different approach? They should be taught that they are a top student because they worked hard, not because they are someone special.

Talk to the child about how they are going to deal with disappointment. Talk to them about how they are going to approach their work every day. Are they are going to approach it with gut-wrenching ferocity, or are they going to approach it casually? The bottom line is that if your child is going to succeed, they must come in with the right attitude when it comes to hard work. If not, they are going to find themselves outperformed by the average student with the above average heart.

Teach them the true meaning of greatness

Many people make the mistake of thinking that "greatness" is a value instilled in a person. We are taught to believe that it is the birthright of some and the wish of many. We talk about "The great Dr. Martin Luther King", or "The great Elvis Presley". What we do not realize is that many of these people were no different from the rest of us before they did great things. In fact, had they spent their lives doing something else, applying less energy or not having the courage to plan and pursue their dreams, they too would be among the many sitting back wishing they possessed the attributes of greatness.

Your potentially complacent child must also understand this lesson. They should be told, loud and clear that their greatness as a student is not something that they were born with, nor is it is a birthright. Greatness is a dynamic process that enters into people sometimes and leaves them at others. Whether it is in you at any given moment depends primarily on whether or not you have chosen to *commit the actions of a great person.* If I were given the choice between being a great man who pretended to be average, or an average man pretending to be great, I would definitely choose the latter.

When it comes to success in college, the great students are the ones who put forth a great effort. That is what makes them extraordinary. In order to be great, you must act great. So, the child should further understand that if they are not putting forth an extraordinary effort on a given day, they are not being the student they think they are. Instead, they are just being average.

This reminds me of a story that I heard from a world famous athlete that I met. He told the story of how he worked so incredibly hard to be a superstar, practicing long after the rest of the team had gone home. He was just a second-rate player attempting to earn some name recognition. Well, he eventually got his recognition. Before long, the national media were stopping him on the street, he was getting millions in salary, and his name was at the center of multi-million dollar corporate endorsement checks. HE HAD MADE IT.

His mistake was that he started to read the press about himself and he also started to believe it. When he would get an award, he felt that the award was given to him because of who he was, rather than what he had done to earn it. He felt that he was *destined* to be the best player on the court, not simply the one who had worked the hardest in practice. So, eventually, he started to get up a little later in the morning. He stopped staying after practice and would leave with the rest of the team. He was then becoming an allegedly great player who behaved as an ordinary one.

Well, the wake-up call was coming. He soon found himself being outplayed by younger, hungrier players. The man eventually recovered from his rift, but this taught him a very important lesson: there is a difference between being the best and being AT YOUR BEST.

Don't accept lower standards!

One of the most common things I see with parents is that they become victims of the college horror stories that people tell them. Because college is so much more challenging than high school (in some ways, it is), they expect their child to head off and come home with grades that are only half as good as they were before. When the child brings back grades that would never have been acceptable in the past, the parent says something like "Well, college is a lot tougher, so we should expect a drop off."

I don't agree with this mentality. We have to remember that like the rats in the lab, if you lower the bar that the student is forced to jump, they are going to give you exactly what you asked for. No, our children are not rats in a lab, but the primary goal of parenthood is to TRAIN another human being. If you let the child off the hook for mediocre grades, they are going to give you mediocrity.

If the child comes home with grades that are not acceptable, you should first help them to assess what happened. How much were they studying? What do they think the problem was? How are they going to improve next semester? How are they going to increase their efforts to the point that they are going to get the results they are used to receiving? This may be a time that they have to pay a higher price for the same commodity.

One of the things you should avoid is the acceptance of lies and lame excuses. If your kids are anything like the ones that I teach, they are going to give you any excuse they can come up with to explain why things didn't work out. Also, like most of us did when we were young, it is never going to be their fault. That is a natural part of growing up, and your role is to help them understand that while some things are out of their control, they cannot go through life with a basketful of excuses.

If they try to tell you something like "I only got a 2.0 GPA, but I was studying 4 hours a day!" That is usually not true. Most students who study consistently every day get "B"s in their courses, unless there are extenuating circumstances.

Then, there is the "My professor is a jerk" excuse. That is when the student says "I would have done well in the course, but the professor was impossible!" While there may be professors that are extremely difficult, many times, a student may choose to blame someone else for their own poor performance. If you are not sure what to think about a particular professor, ask your child what *they* were doing in order to do well in the course. Also, if there were other students who did well in the course, then that means that your child could have done well also. You may also want to compare that grade with the other classes that the child has taken to determine if this is a persistent problem or something that the professor may have caused. The reality is that if a professor is that bad, they are going to get lots of complaints and eventually hear from the dean. The other fact of life is that this might be the time for the child to learn a valuable lesson: we can't always control our boss, but we have to find a way to manage the situation. Having the impression that we can change bosses every time things go wrong on the job is one that can plague us throughout our lives.

Keep the pressure down

Chances are that if you have a reasonably responsible child, they are going to know when they've screwed up. Nagging them into the ground about it is not the way to get them to listen to you. If there are points you want to make, make them once and leave the child alone. The student is already going to feel badly for not performing up to standard.

I recall when I had one "off semester". Like most college students, I had gotten distracted by things outside the classroom, and this led me to not put as much time into my studying as I normally would have. I had gotten a new

120

car, and having the ability to leave campus without taking the bus was quite a powerful feeling. I would ride around town with my music blasting, just having a ball. Well, that semester, my grades showed the effects of my choices. Rather than getting the 4.0 that my parents were accustomed to seeing, they saw a 2.5, which took them back to my days as a pathetic high school student.

Of course I felt terrible. I was incredibly angry at myself, and I swore to myself that I was going to do whatever it takes to get back on top of my school work. My father handled it very well. I recall seeing him next to the fire, as I was walking out the door on my way to campus. He turned toward me and said "You know what you're gonna do, right?" I said "Yes", and that was the end of the conversation. No yelling, no craziness, just my father's look and one sentence.

Well, the following semester was a tremendous comeback story. I earned another perfect grade point average, and even retook two of the courses I had performed poorly in the semester before. I was back on top of my game and my parents were happy about it.

Sometimes, kids can feel bad for what they've done. When they have the right values, they are going to put pressure on themselves to maintain their performance. With as much love as parents have for their kids, it's important to support them and nudge them, but not to push them. This is especially true when they are beyond the age of 18.

Teach them principles

Most of us already teach our children principles and values. There are some values that are incredibly important in college, especially for students combating complacency. These two values are the "Always give more" value, and the ""Get back up" value.

"Always give more" is based upon the premise that most of us do not work equally hard in every situation. Some of us get lazy when things are going really well. Some of us just ball everything up and quit when things are going poorly. There are those who work harder when things are going well, since they are full of confidence and energy from their recent success. There are then those who only work harder when their back is against the wall, they are down to their last breath and their life depends on it. They are fighting for survival. This is the case with many college students, who become Rhodes Scholars when they have a test the following day. Finally, there are those who work harder when they've failed miserably, since they are humiliated by their recent failure and swear to redeem themselves.

What is so irrational about what I just mentioned is that how hard you work should not depend on what just happened to you. The past is the past, and it should be left there. What is interesting is that most of us are affected by the past, even though we would agree that it should have no impact on our choices. So, what is the answer? The solution is simple: no matter what just happened to you, working as hard as you can is ALWAYS the best solution. If the goal is to drive as far as you can in your car, then you are always doing yourself a favor by pushing hard for the next mile.

If you can get your child to buy into this philosophy, they are going to be successful. They will understand that no matter how they did on the last exam or quiz, working harder to prepare for the next one is always the optimal solution. You want them to take as much emotion and disappointment out of the picture as they possibly can. For these emotional problems only take you away from the general prize.

I've always thought about the way you deal with the past as being like a cancer. Imagine someone who has cancer that has spread to their arm. This is a horrible reality to deal with, no doubt about that. This would surely lead the person to reflect on their life, their values, and to feel the sadness that would plague us all in the event that we were confronted with such a daunting reality.

Now, what if the doctor then gives the person more bad news? He says "The cancer has spread through your left arm, very slowly, but deliberately. It is now threatening to expand through the rest of your body. You have one of two choices, either amputate the arm, or die as the cancer spreads itself to your vital organs."

What should the person do? The answer is pretty obvious: they should cut off the bad arm and move forward. Yes, they've lost a great deal in the process, but it's not nearly as terrible as losing your life. You can think of your youth and your time in the same way. Some of us have ruined our past, which, like a cancer, has destroyed a part of our life that we can never get back. The past represents the arm that is already cancerous and recommended for amputation. The other parts of the body, all healthy and clean, represent our future. What is sad is that rather than cutting off the past and letting it go, there are those who hold onto the past and never move forward. They complain about the past, get discouraged and give up on their hopes and dreams. All the while the cancer from the past is slowly but surely destroying their future, because the emotions they feel are causing them to either continue reckless behavior or give up all together.

The smart student is taught to forgive herself when she makes mistakes. That person knows that we all screw up every now and then, and the best thing to do is to let the past go and focus on saving the rest of our lives....the future. Make sure that your child carries this same mentality.

The "Get back up" policy has a different bent than the "Always give more" value. This principle is based upon one simple reality: most great people are miserable failures. What makes this statement true is that when you do something great, you are usually going to fail many times. In fact, the reason that most people do not try to do great things is because of a fear of failure. Those who overcome this fear of failure soon find that this fear is realized, as they fail many times before reaching their prize.

What is also true is that the life of a great person is mostly spent getting up off the floor when faced with one defeat after another. I did not understand any of this as a youth. I thought that all great people simply went through life, accomplishing one great thing after another, not breaking a sweat in the process. I thought that they possessed "It", which I surely did not have. It was "It" that helped them to succeed, while I sat there failing miserably over and over again.

When I was the only African-American in the entire United States to earn a PhD in Finance during the year I graduated, I felt like a failure. Although I had those who told me that I had done something remarkable, I could only think about the many years that I spent trying to climb mountains that seemed too high for me to climb. When I was the top graduating senior in my university, I felt like a failure. Others saw that I had done something special, while I could only think about how much more I could have done if I had not screwed up so many times.

Of course, I have gotten over the feelings I had in the old days. I also realize that going through failure over and over is what made me successful. I still continue to fail, but I now realize that there is tremendous victory in the fact that I continue to try. I only reflect (and this is why I am writing these pages to you) and know that I wish that someone had taught me these lessons at an early age. Had that happened, I would have reached success at a much earlier stage in my life.

Make sure that you instill these values in your child so that they do not find themselves disillusioned once things go wrong (which they will at some point). They have to know that although things are dark, there is light at the end of the tunnel. The problem is that the areas around us can remain dark for a very long time, and it is easy to give up hope or let the illusion convince us that there is nothing else to be obtained.

Getting Your Child Ready for the "Great Freedom Ride"!

"It's no wonder that college students spend much of their time having sex, using drugs and drinking. They've got nothing else to do!" – anonymous college administrator

If I had to think of the greatest thing about college, I would say that it's the freedom! When I think back to my days as a college student, all I can say is "wow". I remember noticing that I could set my schedule whenever I wanted, get up as late as I wanted, go to class if/when I wanted, and stay out as long as I wanted. This was the life! I can also say that this was one of the defining attributes of college that made it much easier for me than high school, which had an incredibly structured setting.

As we all know, freedom can be a double-edged sword. An incredibly fast car can either get you to your destinations faster or get you killed. Fire can burn your food or burn your butt. The sad reality is that many students are simply not prepared to deal with the freedom they experience. I have seen so many students come to college and go bananas that you would think they were part monkey.

Thinking about the parents' role when dealing with college-age students reminds me of a scene in the movie "Bruce Almighty". In the film, Bruce (Jim Carrey) is allowed to take over the powers of God for a few days. One of the frustrations that Bruce runs into is that he is allowed to affect situations, environments and circumstances, but he cannot affect free will. He then asks God "How do I get them to do the right thing without affecting free will?" God then replies "When you find out the answer to that one, let me know."

That conversation might analogize to how parents can sometimes feel about their children when they head off to college. This is an interesting state of flux in the parent-child relationship. The child is still a child, but the child is also an adult. The parent has responsibilities and roles to play in the child's life, and also a certain element of power. At the same time, the parent has to know when to back off and let the child experience life for his/herself. This is a tough balancing act to maintain, for doing too much of one other the other can lead to trouble.

Let them make decisions for themselves

As the parent, your job is not to think for the child forever. The long-run goal is to teach them to think for themselves and make the right decisions. After you've done that, you have to sit back and let them make stupid mistakes. Many parents feel that they need to do everything for their child and make every choice. This is the most crippling, debilitating habit I've ever seen.

I recall being in college, incredibly frustrated by watching my good friend's father drive 80 miles every day to fill out papers for my friend at the Financial Aid office. I remember wondering (as I filled out my own forms) why my friend was not capable of doing his own financial aid paperwork. His father would show up to give him $30, when he could have either mailed the money or told my friend to get a job. I am not sure what kind of dysfunctional relationship they had, but whatever the problem was, my friend felt deep down that he could not make it through college without his dad. As a result, my friend was in college no longer than 1 year. It was not the academics that killed him, it was the fact that he simply felt that he could not make it on his own.

It can be very difficult for us to watch our children make their own choices, especially if we have to sit and watch them make mistakes. But we must understand that while progress has to be made (i.e. they must learn from us), we must also be sure not to cheat them out of the learning process themselves. Also, students can become bitter and resentful when their parents are over controlling and burdening. You become the focus of their anger, and they are more likely to get out of control.

Your child is not your employee

I see many parents that go from the extreme of being too easy on their kids to the other end of the spectrum, in which they feel that because they are paying for college, they have the right to make every choice for their children, and tell them what to do. Their attitude is one in which they seem to feel that like an employer, they are the one that gets to decide how their money is spent. So, they choose the major for the child, they choose the child's courses, they give the child no autonomy to help them to learn the habits of an independent free-thinking adult.

I had a student where her grandparents would force her to come home every single weekend! Like a 10 year old, she would get into the back of the station wagon and go home with her grandparents until the following Sunday. This was her pattern all through the 6 years (yes 6) that it took her to finish college. During all these years, she did not have much of a social life, because she was unable to nurture her friendships during the weekends. Boyfriends would come and go, quickly tiring of seeing her disappear to go home with her grandparents, as if she were a child. Eventually, the girl became lonely and depressed, since she had no friends. She was on psychiatric medication toward the end of her college career, mainly because she felt that she could not thrive on her own. Years later, at the age of

30, this same girl was living with her grandparents, with no plans to move out of the house until/unless she is married. Unfortunately, it is tough to get someone to date you when your grandparents are sitting between the two of you on the couch. Because this young woman never learned independence and her grandparents refused to let go, she is still a child, well into her 30s.

Some parents get confused when they see their children engage in wasteful activities that seem to have no sense of purpose. I am surprised that parents have this reaction, since it is difficult to feel a sense of purpose about something that you had no role in creating. If you were working for a large company in which they never gave you the opportunity to make decisions or choose your role in the company, would you feel that you were a part of the business, or would you feel that you were just a cog in a wheel or a puppet for someone else? Puppets have no sense of purpose. They simply wiggle and move in whatever direction they are shaken. College students can sometimes end up as their parents' puppets. Not knowing why they are doing things, just that they are supposed to do them. The older they get, the more they realize that they don't have to follow parents' orders, the more they are going to rebel. This is just a fact of life.

Teach them the word "Moderation"

When it comes to college and outside activities, there is one pretty simple rule: "If you are doing one thing all the time, then it is probably bad for you." That includes studying. A person who studies 24 hours a day, for example, is going to miss out on much of the growth process that must be incurred to really enjoy college and get something out of it. They are going to leave school as geeks with no social skills, which will hurt them as they try to sell products, see patients, or run businesses in the real world. Intelligence comes in all forms, and social intelligence is just as important as what you learn in the classroom.

Sadly enough, studying is one of the fewest things that students do in excess. Typically, the problems involve things like partying, drinking, video games or just plain old "chillin". The fact that students end up doing things in excess is yet another reminder of how important our habits are in determining what we do with our time. For example, I am a workaholic. I work constantly, all the time. I do it because I love it. It's a high and it is therapeutic for me. When I want to relax, I go into my office, shut the door and don't come out until Jesus comes back from heaven. But there have been other times when I would watch TV to get rid of stress, play basketball or eat ice cream. These coping mechanisms (as psychologists would call them) were based solely on the habits I had formed up until that point. So, you have to have a talk with your child about the habits that they are going to engage in when they start college.

The students who flunk out of college are not simply the ones who party all the time. Those who flunk out might have *happened* to go to a lot of parties, but the parties themselves were not the culprit. It is only when the student goes to parties without studying first that they are in trouble.

I recommend that you remind your child that moderation is extremely important. Remind them that they can do a lot of partying, but they should limit the number of parties they go to, or restrict the partying to only Friday and Saturday nights. You may also want to devise strategies with them regarding how they can get their work done during the day before they go out at night, or how they can free themselves from the things that might tempt them too much. The key to remember is "moderation": that should be the theme word for your child from the very beginning.

If you are aware that your child is doing too much of one thing or another, don't be afraid to step in and simply remind them that they may want to slow down. Most parents know their children's habits, and when things just don't seem right, we can "smell" the fact that they are probably doing something outside the norm. If you sense this, either by the grades you see or from talking to your child, go ahead and at least "put a bug in their ear". You can also try little things like calling them on Saturday and Friday nights to see if they are home, or calling them early on Saturday and/or Sunday morning to get a sense for how late they were out the night before.

You can also pick up on whether your child is engaged in moderation by listening to them. If you are more likely to hear your child talk to their friends about the next party than about the next exam, that could be a problem. If you see them cramming like crazy before every test, that could be a sign that they are not studying properly. If you ask them when their next exam is coming and they have no idea, that could be a problem as well. Keep an eye on your child's habits, for that can provide a lot of very helpful clues.

An ounce of prevention

As you pay attention to your child's outcomes throughout the semester, keep tabs on them. Notice how hard they are studying. Ask them about their courses and grades. Since you paying the bills, you certainly have a right to know.

Many universities do not allow anyone, even parents, to know how their child's grades are coming along. That is part of the privacy policy. I admit that this doesn't make a lot of sense to me, since I believe that the person paying the bills should have the right to see what they are getting for their money. But just because the university does not allow you to go through them to get the information doesn't mean that your child can impose the same rule upon you. Especially if you are paying the bills, you have the right to ask your child at any time how their courses are going. Try to get specifics. Don't say "How's English?" Say things like "So, what did you get on that quiz?" If they didn't perform well, they are going to be Houdini-like in their tactics of deception.

You may even want to go as far as asking your child to get a progress report from every professor in the middle of the semester. I, for example, am happy giving progress reports to students. I cannot give them to their parents, but if your child gets a report from me, there is nothing wrong with your asking the child to give you what I just gave him/her. I have also seen parents who simply come visit the child in the middle of the semester, asking to meet with all their professors. That is a good way to find out the truth about how things are going in the classroom. The child is not likely to deny your request, and it is going to be difficult for them to tell you a lie if the professor is standing right there.

The slow, winding road of academic misery

Finding out too late is a common problem that parents run into with their students. We don't hear that the biology class is going poorly until the final exam. Or, you keeping hearing the letter "B" all semester, until that "B" slowly transforms into an "F". There are times when students are just flat out deceptive toward their parents, keeping their grades from them for fear that they are going to get "chewed out". There are also the more common cases, however, during which the students themselves have no idea how the class is going.

Missy was a freshman in college, a great student in high school. She had a very high GPA and an equally amazing ACT score, so she was prepared for college. During her first semester, she was ill for one week and forced to miss class. She missed a quiz, but was diligent when it came to "touching base" with her professor about what she had missed. The professor then told Missy not to worry about the quiz, and her grade was "Fine, about a B-ish".

Taking her professor's word, Missy went on as if everything were OK. What she did not know was that in preparation for the final exam, the professor had given some privileged information out during class, the kinds of things that are not in the textbook. Additionally, missing this quiz did indeed hurt Missy's grade. When her professor told her that she didn't have to worry about the quiz, what he actually meant was that she could miss the quiz and still pass the class. He didn't mean that she would get the "A" or "B" that she expected. Also, the quiz might have been OK to miss only because the professor allows all students to drop their lowest quiz grade. So, her lowest quiz grade was now a zero, meaning that all other quizzes were going to count. So, Missy does poorly on the final exam, and the fact that she missed a quiz means that she is going to have all of her quizzes counted, including her lowest score. She ends the semester with a D-minus.

The story about Missy is not uncommon in college and the communication gap between a professor and student can take many different forms. Sometimes it is completely the student's fault, and sometimes it is the professor's fault. In most cases, both parties share some part of the blame.

What you should know about professors

The first thing you should remember about professors is that we have a lot of students. An "acceptable" grade in our minds is one that is higher than the average, which might be a C+. So, any student that has a B-minus average is considered a good student, even if that person has a 4.0 grade point average. That means that if we say "You're doing ok in my class", that might mean that you are doing better than the average. When you come to us complaining that you got a horrible grade, you may hear us say something like "What do you mean? You did better than most of the other students!"

Secondly, the professor's calculation is usually going to be highly imprecise. When your child hears something like "You're doing fine." What they are really hearing might be what the professor needs to tell them to get that person out of their office. "Doing fine" can mean a lot of different things to different people, so if there are no more questions asked, then no more answers are usually given. The best way for your student to deal with this is to ask for *specifics*. You have a right to have the professor calculate your grade explicitly to tell you exactly where you stand. You should have your child get this calculation and then have the calculation forwarded onto you.

Third, even if the professor is completely forthcoming about the grading situation, the student may be the one that is lost. College can be hugely deceptive: you can think that everything is fine for the longest time, then when you least expect it - WHAM! You find out that your grade is in the toilet. The bomb may be from pure miscalculation, or it may come from the fact that one bad test score can quickly change a good grade into a bad one.

This subtle deception is something that you should discuss with your child. You should teach them the warning signs they can use to figure out how well they are doing in class, even if there is no homework being given to them every night. Professors can make the student feel that everything is going great, and by the time the student finds out, it might be too late.

Your child should be taught to calculate their own grade and keep their own records for the entirety of any course that they take. Yes, professors do lose assignments, and yes, they make many grading errors. The student who has no proof that they actually turned in quiz #2 is the one that will have to accept the zero. The students that keep track of their own grades are the ones who keep the professors on their toes.

The key for you as a parent is to teach your child these techniques BEFORE they set foot on campus. The 4 years of college go by very quickly, and some mistakes can be huge and costly. By the time certain lessons are learned, the game is over. If your child is aware of the process in advance of other students, they are going to be at a tremendous advantage.

Don't forget your rights

While I mention earlier that your children are not your employees, I am not meaning to say that you don't have any rights. It is my opinion that a good college parent holds their child responsible for their actions. You can check who they are living with, what they are doing with their time, why their grades were not up to par, etc. Many of these rights belong to you, and it helps the university community when parents use these rights effectively.

When you find that your child is not using their time the way that you would like for them to, you always have the option of cutting certain types of financial support. I am not one to say that it is wrong to take money away from students who are not using their parents' money wisely. It may sound rough, but the reality is that most of us spend our lives paying attention to those who hold the purse strings. If we do not do what our boss wants us to do, we are going to get fired. An unhappy customer means that we are not going to get their business again. So, why should students not learn these lessons early?

Why goal setting is important

Every student should arrive to college with the ability to set goals. It is part of your job as a parent to teach them goal-setting and how to go from the conceptual stage of setting goals to the other stages that lead to goal fulfillment. Goal setting is incredibly important because this also gives the student the chance to feel that they are a part of their growth process. They feel empowered and are filled with a sense of purpose. If you set the goals for your child and then tell them what to do, they will feel detached from the objective and unwilling to work for it.

Let me give you a quick and dirty break down of how I perceive the goal-setting process. This is the way that you might want to explain it to your child. You can first break the process into 3 types of goals: Long, medium and short-range. The different types of goals are not distinct, they are part of the same function, the same way that a brick is a piece of a wall, which is a piece of a building. Every short-range goal should go toward the fulfillment of a medium range goal, which helps to reach the long-range goal.

Setting all 3 types of goals is critical for college students, since most of them do not have the ability to focus on a long-range objective on a daily basis. This is one of the reasons that students struggle with the fact that many college classes only have one test each month, with nothing in between. Setting short-term goals gives them a daily and weekly feedback process that will let them know if they are getting off track.

Here are what I would argue to be the steps in the goal-setting process:

1) Setting the goal itself
2) Setting a strategy to achieve the goal.
3) Executing the strategy
4) Implementing a feedback evaluation mechanism to determine if you are on track to reach the objective.

I can best outline this goal-setting process with the following example. Assume that my goal is to ride my bike from New York to California, arriving there within the next 2 weeks.

1) **Setting the goal:** the goal is simple. I want to be sitting on the beach within the next two weeks. This is what I would call a long-range goal, since several short-range goals can be created in the process.

2) **Setting the strategy to achieve the goal:** "I have to drive 3,000 miles within 14 days. I am going to have to do at least 215 miles per day on average. That is going to require me, at 60 mph, to drive about 3.5 – 4 hours every single day." This part of the goal-setting process is crucial, because this is how the students learn what they *must do every single day* to reach their objective. When they falter and come up short on a given day, they are going to know that they are off track. This keeps the mind from playing tricks on you.

3) **Executing the strategy:** This is, without question, the most difficult part of the goal-setting process. Any fool can have a dream. Any other fool can even set a strategy to accomplish the dream. But it is the *execution* that separates the small number of MDs from the many millions of people who felt that they were going to have an MD one day in the future. If a person has the ability to execute all things that they plan, they can conquer the world.

I have no doubt that you want your child to be a warrior and a high achiever. If so, you should teach them to put their money where their mouth is. That means they should be shown the goal setting

140

process in its' entirety and have it explained to them in such a way that they can achieve all of these realistic objectives.

The importance of the execution process is supplemented by the process of daily renewal. We are not always going to be our best every day. Sometimes, our children can go to the other extreme and be incredibly hard on themselves when they don't succeed or reach their short-term goals. You should remind them that every day is new and distinct from the day before. What was not done in the past can be achieved in the future. That is how they are taught to stick with their agenda and continue the execution process, even when things don't go right.

4) **Implementing the feedback mechanism:** This is where the driver analyzes herself every day to determine if she is doing what she needs to do to reach her goal. She might imagine an "on-track version" of herself; someone who has driven the correct number of miles. She can then compare herself every couple of days to this person. If she is ahead of her, she is doing well. If she is behind, she needs to speed up or drive a little longer each day. The idea is that there is a constant self-monitoring process that will drive her toward her goals. Without such a mechanism, it would be very easy to get distracted, thinking that everything is ok, only to find yourself at the deadline with another 1,000 miles to go.

The wisdom of life

One persistent difference I've noticed between students is that some students are wiser than others. While many of them get to college and seem to be normal 18 year olds, there are wildly varying degrees to which each student knows what to do in their new environment. While there are some students that know that drinking too much is a bad thing, there are some who think that they should turn themselves into a human toilet. Typically, the defining factor is how much guidance they've received before their arrival.

If/when your child heads to a college campus, you may want to spend some time giving them some age-old words of wisdom. Many times, they may not seem to be listening, but you never know when something you tell them is going to come in handy during a tough situation. A lot of students make stupid mistakes because they simply don't know. Think about your own life and times when you've done dumb things that you wouldn't do now. Sometimes, it was a matter of your having to do it to learn that it wasn't right for you, but many times, we make mistakes because we simply don't know what is going on. If you can assist your child in learning life and maturity before they arrive on campus, they are probably going to be better off.

One tactic that I've seen used is to allow the child to talk to two older people: one who has made the "right" choices, and one who has not. You would be surprised at how much both of these people agree with one another when it comes to doing the right thing. But the person who made the mistakes can give the most credible advice, since that person is the one who suffered the consequences of their actions. I learned many lessons by talking to those who were able to tell me what not to do, and that gave me a great deal of wisdom at an early age. Wisdom is what gives the student the courage to know that some choices are smart and others are not.

You may also want to let your child talk to recent college graduates. Let the graduates tell them the good and bad things about college, things to watch out for, pitfalls, etc. Hearing these things in advance will at least ensure that if they make the mistake later, they can't say that it was because they were not warned.

Time is More Valuable Than Money, Teach This To Your Kids First!

"I never understood how my daughter could say that she didn't have time to get ready for her finals. She doesn't even have a job!" – anonymous parent.

As a professor of Finance, you can imagine that I get excited when I talk about money. Most of us think that money is important, at least important enough to manage. But many of us are not careful with our time. Wasting time is worse than wasting money, because time is more valuable than money. If you lose $1,000, you can go work and get it back. But if you waste the year that you are 18, you will never be 18 again. The sooner a kid can learn this in college, the better off they are going to be.

Most students manage their time the way that our government seems to manage the budget: with huge deficits and insane amounts of spending. They end the day the way many of us did at that age, wondering where all the time went. Before they know it, the exam is staring them in the face, and they are suddenly way up a creek. I have some thoughts on ways that you can teach your child to manage their time as they head off to college.

The Free Cash Flow Theory

The Free Cash Flow Theory is a goofy financial theory that I learned in graduate school. While the theory might be goofy, it does have a meaningful application in this context. It basically says that if a company has a bunch of extra money sitting around, it is going to waste it. So, what you can do to keep the company from wasting money is to make them take on debt or some other financial obligation that is going to take the money out of their hand. Paying the interest on the debt keeps the company's managers from having the money just sitting around, so they cannot use it making bad investments and buying more corporate jets.

I guess, on the surface, the theory makes sense. It's kind of tough to waste something if you don't have it sitting around to throw away. But maybe instead of incorrectly applying it to financial theory, we could have applied it to college students.

Many parents do too much for their kids in college, opening up all their time for studying. They think that their child is away at college hitting the books like Muhammad Ali on a punching bag. While students do study, they spend a lot of time wasting time. This is because it's easy to waste time when you've got another 2 weeks until your next exam. What are you going to do, start studying now or wait another week? Some students do the right thing, but most will just take their time.

So, if you want your child to manage their time, you should create conditions that will force the child to see time as a scarce commodity. Check to see if they are involved in constructive extracurricular activities. Maybe force them to get a job. For some reason, many parents see it as a crime to make their child work. *Working builds character.* My students that work are VOLUMES more responsible than those who do not. Think about your own life. How productive would you be if you could sit around and wait for someone to send you money every month? Wouldn't that just make you a welfare recipient? Do you want your child to be a welfare recipient? Of course you don't.

You don't have to force your child to work full time, although many students do. Working forty hours per week, while it might seem criminal, can be managed, and can be a good way to prepare for the real world. But only working, say, 20 hours per week might be just enough to keep them productive.

147

When I speak to kids across the country about time management, I break it down for them in this way: I mention that there are 168 hours in a week. If a person gets a full night of sleep, 8 hours, that leaves them with 112 hours (168 – 56) to do other things. If they are in class for 15 hours per week, that leaves them 97 hours. If they spend 2 hours per day on personal hygiene, they are going to have 83 hours leftover. That means that the student can work 40 hours per week and have another 43 hours left for studying, parties, etc. If the student works 20 hours per week, they have 63 hours: they can use 40 hours for studying (enough to do pretty well in their classes, since most students don't study 40 hours per week), and the last 23 hours for Xbox games, parties, etc. Imagine if you don't make your child work. That means that the student is going to have 83 HOURS of free time every week! That's nearly 12 hours a day! So, for half their lives, they are going to be allowed to sit around doing nothing if they choose to do so.

They certainly are not going to study for the entire 12 hours they have free every day. The easy temptation is to do what all "time rich" people do: they are going to waste a bunch of it. Once you get into the habit of wasting time, it is difficult to suddenly tighten your belt. Remember: An idle schedule is the Devil's workshop. The *likelihood that your child is going to get into mischief is greater if they have nothing else to do.*

The point in this exercise is not to tell people what to do. It's to remind them that they have options. They may think that they don't have any time, but they are alive and breathing for the same number of hours as their classmates. The difference between those who get a lot done and those who do not is the ability to manage their time.

The final point I would like to make about forcing your child to get a job is the fact that I get tired of seeing parents sending their kids so much money! As a Finance Professor, I actually make a nice salary. But I have many students wearing clothing that I will never be able to afford. I am not jealous, for out-dressing me is not a difficult achievement. But I wonder to myself "What drives this kid?" If luxury is handed to them, do they have anything to which they would like to aspire? I recall knowing that my education was going to give me the chance to live a better life, under my own steam. Had my parents sent me hundreds of dollars every month to live a comfortable life, I would never have been able to focus. I would not have been hungry. I would not have achieved so much. Don't take this hunger away from your child by giving them everything before they have a chance to work for it.

If the child keeps slipping, let them taste the real world

Think for a second about your own life. When did you really learn the value of a dollar? When did you really learn the value of your time? When did you really learn the value of your opportunities? Was it when time, money and opportunities were readily available, or was it when you suddenly found yourself scrambling to find more time, money was short, and your life seemed to be covered with brick walls blocking your progress? Most of us might agree that the earlier we learn these lessons, the better off we are. This is sometimes true even if the lessons were very painful and difficult to learn. Also, years later, we look back and have the most affection toward those who helped us learn those lessons, even if we were not appreciative at the time.

If your child is not using their opportunities the way that they should, there is nothing wrong with letting them feel the brunt of what you are going through to get them through school. Having them pay their own bills for a while would most likely build a sense of appreciation within them, as well as a new sense of determination as they suddenly realize that these opportunities do not come for free.

I once had a very bright student, one who was expected to do extremely well in college. He arrived with a very high ACT score and grade point average, but he was unfocused. During his freshman year, he joined a fraternity. This began his travels down the wrong path. One thing led to another, and he was eventually spending much more time at parties and hanging out than he was studying. He came to class about once a month, and he failed my course. He also ended up failing the courses of all of his professors, earning a horribly low grade point average in the process. This was sad to me, because I knew the kind of promise he had. I also knew his father, a physician, who had paid a great deal of money for him to attend such an expensive university. Eventually, the student was kicked out of school, since his grade point average was below the university minimum. He left school, and his father forced him to feel the consequences of his actions. While he was allowed to come back home, he was forced to get a job and pay rent while he was there. There was no reason, his father felt, for him to be over the age of 18 and to get the chance to live rent-free. This was not how the world worked. He then told him that in order to live with him, he had to enroll in school. He also forced him to pay his own tuition with the money he earned from his job. He wasn't able to get into a 4-year college, since his prior grades were so low. So, his father let him feel the humiliation of going to junior college.

The young man's attitude changed immediately. He began to realize his potential, and before long, he was the top student at his community college. He later went on to a 4-year college, earning a nearly perfect grade point average. Additionally, he never asked his parents for money again, since he had learned the value of independence. He eventually pursued graduate school, and went on to have a wonderful career.

The student I mentioned above is one that benefited from the tough love that his parents administered onto him. Had his parents continued to coddle him, he never would have matured. He thanks his parents to this day for forcing him to go through such a wonderful, yet volatile learning experience. This would be better than having him learn the same lessons at the age of 45.

Whose Loan is it anyway?

I have always been amazed when I see parents take on tens of thousands of dollars in debt for their children, as if their children are simply incapable of making the payments themselves. Many parents, somehow convinced that their child is not old or mature enough to have student loans, or perhaps feeling an extreme amount of guilt for letting their children start their careers in debt, end up borrowing lots of money so that their children can go to college. This debt is taken on in addition to already high mortgages, pending retirement, and all the other major financial hurdles that the American family must face. I find this amazing.

I personally borrowed a great deal to go to college, but I wouldn't change a thing. I felt good about my choice, because my parents were not burdened with paying my loans in addition to their other financial obligations. With the amount I was forced to borrow, my parents would have been paying my loans for the next 20 years, which would have been ironic since I made more money than both of them put together.

Nurturing and supporting your child does not mean treating them as if they are incapable. If you treat them as if they are incapable, they will remain incapable. While life would have been easier if I could have had my parents repay my loans, I would never have learned many valuable lessons of financial responsibility. Do not rob your child of these lessons.

A nice compromise might be taking on some small percentage of the loan, like a fourth. That way, you can show the child that you care without doing everything for them. But I also see no problem with letting the child assume full responsibility for the loan, so that they learn the value of making a long-term investment. Nearly every great corporation in America was founded with debt, so their career does not need to be an exception.

Teach them to account for their time

The same way that a person should account for what they did with their money, a student should be taught to account for what they've done with their time.

I can give you an example:

When I had only been teaching at the collegiate level for 3 years, I recall meeting the parents of one of my students. The mother told me that she was baffled regarding why her daughter was bringing home such horrible grades. She and her daughter both claimed that she was studying 6 – 8 hours per day, 7 days a week, and that she was not even able to get a job, since she was studying so much.

While I cannot say that I could read anyone's mind, I felt in my heart that the student was fibbing or at least not aware of where her time was going. I knew that if someone studied that much, they typically were not going to get bad grades. In fact, they would probably be one of the best students in the class.

I told the mother that not only did I think that her daughter could do better in school, but she could also get a job. I believed that her daughter only suffered from a time management problem, nothing more.

*One day, during class, I asked the daughter what she was "up to". She said that she had slept until 11, came right to class, been in class for 3 hours, was going home to take a nap, then going to her boyfriend's house, and coming home after that. **Not once did she mention the idea of studying**. I thought to myself "Hmmm, it would seem that a person who studies 6 – 8 hours per day would have mentioned studying someplace in that paragraph".*

When I mentioned my observation about the girl's statement,, she froze. I didn't push her into a corner, but I told her that I find it ironic that she doesn't have time to make better grades, she can't get a job, and that she spends 6 – 8 hours per day studying, yet she doesn't mention studying as one of her primary daily activities. When most of us have a job that takes up 8 hours of our day, we are going to be quite likely to mention the job when someone asks us what we were doing that day.

The girl didn't say much, she only tried to back peddle. She explained to me that she forgot to mention that she was going to study with her boyfriend (Yeah, right. We know how those study sessions go, don't we?), and that she was going to get some work done during the 2 hours before heading to his house. No matter how you sliced and diced it, however, there was no way that she could find 8 hours of study time during the busy schedule that she described to me.

I didn't tell the young lady what to do. Kids tend to hate it when you tell them what to do. I only made a suggestion. I told her that when I was in school, I would sometimes think that I worked harder than I actually did. I didn't realize where my time was going until I sat down and figured out where it was. I then went on to explain to the girl how to put together a "Time Budget" and find out what she was doing with her spare time.

I noticed that within two weeks, the girl's grades improved dramatically. She also informed me within the month that she had gotten a part-time job. I was later informed that she took my comments to heart and tried to figure out where her time was going. She was shocked to find out how much spare time she was wasting. Her feeling was analogous to the financial magic that people show when they tell you how much money you would have at the end of the year if you save the money that you spend on coffee. It was incredibly interesting.

The moral to this story is quite simple: if you want to know what your child is doing with their time, encourage them to first find out what they are doing before they tell you. Chances are that they are going to tell you whatever will get them through the day, since many times, they themselves have no idea what they are doing. They don't realize until they are older that if you sit motionless for long periods of time, you are going to find out soon that your entire day has been wasted, and you have not moved an inch.

Drinking, Drugs and All the Other Collegiate Vices

"It wasn't until I woke up the next morning that the police officer taking me in told me that someone had been raped in the next room. I was still in trouble, even though I passed out long before it happened." – anonymous college student.

One of the hardest things about college is that while it can be a wonderful place, it can be extremely dangerous. This is sad for me, for I've seen student after student come to college as a naïve Freshman, only to leave as something much more frightening years later. This makes me sad, for I could see their potential going down the drain. It is my personal mission to help parents and students learn what they need to know to be equipped to battle this serious problem.

Alcoholism is one of the worst problems on college campuses today. According to the National Institute of Alcohol Abuse and Alcoholism, alcohol is responsible for 1,400 student deaths per year, and 500,000 unintentional injuries. Many of these problems are due to the campus culture, which teaches kids that drinking until you pass out is just a part of "getting along in college".

I personally worked my way around this culture. I knew at an early age from watching relatives have problems with alcohol that this was not a good thing. It also helped that I've always found the taste of liquor to be disgusting. But my friends were not the same way. I had a very good friend who started drinking when we first began college. He joined a fraternity that encouraged drinking, and before long, he was gone. He was a smart guy and a very good student, but we were very different when it came to alcohol.

My friend would get drunk every Thursday, and it seemed that he would not get sober again until the following Sunday. This was his typical pattern, since his fraternity "brothers" were always encouraging him to do things that were clearly not part of his personality. If anything, he was an incredibly meek person most of the time. But when he was with "his boys", he turned into someone else. I was disappointed with his actions, for I think that there was something missing in his self-esteem that led him to feel the need for acceptance from others.

He was a bright individual, so he ended up earning admission to a very good law school. He eventually became an attorney, a successful one. However, the drinking problems never left him. He now lives his life as yet another alcoholic attorney, going to AA meetings between court dates. His life is very sad, with divorce after divorce, and one drinking binge after another. All this started in college.

The story about my friend is extremely typical on college campuses. Many students start off on the right foot, and then end up on the wrong foot of life. College is one of the most powerful ways to begin the process of ruining your life forever.

Prepare your kids for this stuff before they leave for campus

You probably want to sit and have one of those uncomfortable conversations with your child long before they come to a college campus. If you don't, they are going to get their information from another 18-year old (pretty scary, isn't it?) The culture on college campuses is one where alcohol and other vices lie around every corner, and it's up to you to explain to them the consequences of these choices.

You want the child to know that just because everything seems ok on campus, it is not. It is easy for many students to think that just because they are on a college campus, the things that affect everyone else are not going to affect them. They believe that they can drink every weekend and never get addicted. They think that because their friends use a certain type of drug, that it must be Ok. The list goes on and on. I have seen very good kids get caught up in all the wrong things, only to ruin their lives forever.

You may consider letting them talk to someone who has recently finished college, or someone who is close to the end. That person, if they are a responsible student, is likely to explain the things that go on and how to keep from letting them nab you when you get there. They may be more likely to listen to that person than to listen to you. But no matter how they receive the message, it only matters that they get it.

You may also want to give them a serious reality check. That might mean showing them the opposite side of things: letting them meet someone who made all the *wrong* choices in college. This can be an even more powerful lesson, since that person is likely to regret their decisions in college. I have found that young people can be more persuaded by these testimonials than the good ones. There is usually nothing more powerful than someone in prison saying "Don't do what I did."

As part of the reality shock, you may try to arrange a tour of a jail or rehab clinic. You could also consider taking a visit to AA and talking to one of the counselors. Specifically, you may ask the counselor to talk about college students and binge drinking. That will make the experience more real for the child. I would also recommend having a visit to the campus and talking with professors and administrators who can give your child an update on the things that tend to plague college students the most.

The key to this information is that you want your child to be informed. If they are not informed, then it is a lot more difficult to get angry at them when they make the wrong decisions. You would be amazed at how uninformed 18-year olds can be, even on the simple things.

Do not accept "tradition" if it does not make sense

I am shocked at times to see how many parents simply accept the fact that heavy drinking is part of the college tradition. Perhaps some of the parents themselves engaged in heavy drinking as students, so they consider it just part of growing up.

While I cannot say that drinking in itself is a horrible thing, I can say that parents should realize that the fact that everything turned out OK does not make the decision a good one. That is important to know. I have seen very good students who don't even drink very much have horrible things happen to them when they found themselves consuming alcohol heavily. In fact, I knew of a student who was *raped 4 times during college*, all of which took place while she was too drunk to realize what was going on. Many of these incidents are not reported, and their parents never have a clue. I pray that your child does not have to go through this kind of thing, and I hope that you will do what you can to ensure that they do not.

The growth of Gambling

What is also interesting is the surge of gambling on college campuses. Millions of students across the U.S. find themselves addicted to gambling. What starts off as a few friendly bets grows into something far less tolerable. This reminds me of a story about a student I once knew:

Jack went to a new friend, Billy's house on a Saturday afternoon to watch some football games. He was with his other friend, Joe, their mutual acquaintance. Jack and Billy immediately became friends, bonding over sporting events throughout the day. At one point, Jack notices that Billy is making a phone call, saying something about "the point spread" for the next game. He asks about the call and is told by Billy that he had just made a call to "his bookie". Jack loves sports, so he wants "a piece of the action". He places a $50 wager on the next game for his favorite team to "beat the spread" (score more points against the other team than expected).

Two hours later, Jack has won $50. He places another bet, this time for $100. He wins again. He is excited over the fact that he won more money in 5 hours than he would have earned all week on his job. He also loves to predict basketball games anyway, so he figures that this would be a great way to make easy cash.

Jack eventually finds himself going to his friend Billy's house on a regular basis. They become good buddies, with gambling as their common bond. In fact, he eventually stops going to the house and starts making phone calls to place bets. After a while, he cuts the middleman completely and starts to call the bookie himself.

As you can guess, Jack's luck eventually turns against him. He finds himself making heavy bets and enduring heavy losses. Each time he losses, he feels deep down that he can make all of his money back with "one good score". No such luck. Jack eventually finds himself owing the bookie $1400.

Jack is worried about paying the bookie, since he doesn't have the money. What is worse is that even though he has incurred huge losses, he never stops gambling. He eventually finds ways to pay his debts illegally, like writing bad checks to his credit card companies, or even stealing. Eventually, Jack is over his head in debt, worried about what is going to happen when the bookie finds out that he cannot pay him.

The bookie is impatient with Jack, for his gambling debt has grown to over $8,000. To scare Jack into paying, the bookie tells him that if he doesn't pay, he is going to stab his mother. He recites Jack's home address to let him know that he is serious. Not knowing what to do, Jack commits suicide.

The story above is, unfortunately, not as uncommon as you might think. Just like toddlers, students with a lot of free time on their hands have incredibly creative ways of getting themselves into serious trouble. That is just a fact.

One of the solutions is to make your child aware of these problems that exist. If they don't know that gambling can get them into trouble, they may not be smart about it. Secondly, you have to have the channels of communication wide open, so that if they do screw up, they will talk to you about it. One other unfortunate thing about kids is that they, like Jack, can sometimes find permanent solutions to temporary problems, which is not what you want them to do.

Gambling is turning into a huge problem, one that rivals that of alcohol abuse. A study by The University of Minnesota reports that 19% of all male students, and 5% of all female students report gambling daily or weekly[i]. Therefore, at some point, your child is likely to meet someone who gambles.

What is also interesting is that it has been found that students who have a lot of extra time and money on their hands are those that are most likely to gamble[ii]. So, this would argue that limiting your child's spare time and money might be a good way to keep them from having gambling problems. You may even want to have them send receipts for the things that you help them pay for, or perhaps pay for these things directly. A student with a gambling problem is certain to call with many invisible expenses being paid by an unwitting parent. Don't let that parent be you.

Ways to monitor your child's behavior

It is tough to keep tabs on your child when they head to college, but there might be ways to get some idea of what is going on with them. Perhaps you can just listen to their conversations to see what kinds of topics they tend to discuss the most.

- Are they more likely to call friends about studying or to call them about going to yet another party?

- If you call the child at 10:30 AM on a Sunday morning, are they still asleep, or are they up at the library?

- If you ask them how classes are going, do they give you specific answers, or just generic ones that imply that they themselves have no clue what is going on?

- What mindset do their friends have? Are they productive students or people that look like they are fresh out of rehab?

- If you tell the child that you are going to make a surprise visit, how do they react?

- If you ask them about drinking, what do they say? Do they say "never" or "occasionally"? This might help you zone in on their drinking habits.

While these suggestions are not sure-fire, some of them are likely to give you an indication of how your child is using their educational opportunities. You should in some ways, respect their privacy, while at the same time, realize that you are also a part of this process. They are looking to you for guidance.

Sex: The Great Extracurricular

"I had sex with 200 women this year alone." – anonymous student, bragging about his sexual exploits.

Yep, kids have sex. We did it, and they are going to do it. That is just the way that God meant for it to be. I am not here to tell you what your family policy should be when it comes to sexual activity. I am only here to share ideas which, based on my experience, can help you to make your child aware of the consequences of their sexual behavior.

According to a 1997 survey by the Center for Disease Control, 79.5% of all college students reported having sex, with over half of them admitting to having had sex in the past 30 days[iii]. What is even more telling about this statistic is that 20 – 25% of all college students get a sexually transmitted disease at some point during their college career. The most common diseases on college campuses are HPV (Human Papillomavirus) or genital warts, Chlamydia, and genital herpes[iv]

What you should also realize is that in spite of the fact that we have some of the scariest STDs in human history circulating in our society, a shocking 79% of all college students report having had unprotected sex at some point during their college career![v] This blows my mind, since it shows that kids really are incredibly uninformed before they arrive to college. The information that the rest of us take for granted are things that many college students have yet to learn.

You have to make sure that your child is not in the uninformed boat. A survey by Men's Health Magazine showed that 35% of all students reported not using condoms at all. I think that this estimate is a bit high, but it's alarming nonetheless. Also, a vast majority of students are not able to identify the woman's most fertile period of the month.

Have a conversation with your child about the birds and the bees before they head to college. If you can't do it yourself, then have someone that you both respect discuss the issue with the student. It could be the most important conversation they've ever had.

Teach them the value of moderation

Chances are that your child is not going to talk to you about what they are doing in the bedroom. To this day, it would be tough for me to even *admit* to my mother that I've had sex! So, this could be a delicate discussion. However, you should realize that even if the child acts like they are not listening to what you are saying, there is a good chance that they are absorbing the information. So, I encourage you to just put it out there and then let them have it at their disposal if they want to use it. I can think of many times when my mother swore that I wasn't listening to anything she was saying, but I remembered it all. Years later, something would happen in which the information came in handy, and I would use it. That is just how kids work.

The thing that you should tell your kids is that while you may or may not have a problem with them having sex, they should at least value and respect the sexual process. That means that you at least encourage them to not be the kind of student that puts their sexual organs into use at every available opportunity. Promiscuity is a huge problem on campuses, and it contributes to the spread of disease. So, while your child may still choose to have sex, at least they will be persuaded to be monogamous.

Being a Virgin and Proud of It

Remember when I mentioned that 79% of all college students have sex? Well, that means that 1 in 5 do not. Your child could be that one. It is going to take some self-confidence for them to remain in that category and part of that self-confidence is going to come from you. If you suspect that your child is a virgin, you should explain to them why that is a good thing and something of which they should be proud. This confidence you instill in them is going to come in handy later when they deal with the peer pressure from that person who may or may not want to be with them because of their sexual choices.

It is not my goal to say that abstinence is better than being sexually active. However, it is certainly my goal to make you feel proud of who you are. If your child chooses to abstain, make sure they feel good about it. Many students make this choice, and they are usually better off because of it.

Teaching them how the opposite sex operates (Sharing your wisdom)

Most of us who have dealt with the opposite sex for long periods of time know that there are good and bad people in this world. There is the guy who wants to love you for a lifetime, and then there is the guy who wants try to give you a lifetime of love in one night. There are the women that are loyal and supportive, and then there are those who are loyal until you lose your job.

Most of us learn how the opposite sex operates over time. The less mentorship that a child receives, the more they are going to have to go through the hard knocks of life in order to learn the lessons that many of us already know. You might want to spend some time with your child explaining how the opposite sex operates. This conversation should be candid and honest, with very little sugar coating. Life doesn't sugar coat reality, so you shouldn't either.

You may want your female child to know that some guys are flat out liars and sex hounds. This is especially true in college, where some guys take pride in the number of sexual conquests they can attain in a short period of time. Many of these conquests are attained through deception, and freshmen girls are the easiest targets. Even worse, there are rapists who take advantage of young women that trust them before they've truly earned their trust. You should do your best to explain these things to your child before they head to campus.

On the male side, I personally have been deceived at times by those whom I believed to be loyal. Guys might make financial mistakes, where you over-invest in the woman that you think is going to be with you forever, only to have reality smack you in the face like a baseball bat. These can be trying and difficult experiences, and I know that I went through my share.

One of the biggest mistakes that students make is that when they go through the drama of relationships, they can sometimes get distracted. Getting that girl or guy back into your arms becomes more important than anything else in the world, including studying. That is sad, because years later, the student has to look at the horrible grades they earned that semester when they went through the difficult process of breaking up.

While some of these experiences are simply things that we must go through to understand, there are a lot of mistakes that can be avoided if there is someone there to explain to us how they work. Also, the love that the child feels they are missing from their lost mate can be partially mediated by love they feel they are getting from their parents. Remind them that their friends and family are going to be with them permanently, long after the guy or girl they are lusting for is gone.

Promoting Good Sexual Health

If your child is sexually active, they should definitely see a physician on a regular basis. This visit should of course include the Pap smear and an HIV test. Most universities have health clinics that the student can visit, and since they are not likely to share things with you, it is important that your child understand the necessity of taking care of these issues on their own.

If there is a question of pregnancy, Planned Parenthood is usually nearby. Again, you might be one of the last to know if there is a pregnancy scare. So, it's important the child is self-automated when it comes to knowing how to calm herself in the event that she is witnessing the wrong color on the pregnancy test.

Planned Parenthood is also a good place to get free condoms and good sex education. Your child should be made aware of this. Your child should also be made clearly aware of the fact that they should never engage in intercourse without using a condom. You may think they already know this, but they should be reminded just in case.

If you find out that they've made a sexual mistake, try not to kill them right away. The more panicked you are, the less likely they are to talk to you in the future. At the same time, you have to let them know that there are expectations for them as they head off to college, and your job is not just to send money and sit idly by the side.

Supporting Your Child as They Go through Academic Hardship

"I never thought my college GPA would be literally one half of the one I got in high school" – College sophomore as he came close to flunking out.

As much as we hate to think about it, there may come a time when your child struggles academically. The sad reality is that there are times when even the most well prepared parents have children that struggle in college. This can happen to anyone, and the best we can all hope for is that the issues are temporary.

Don't be so quick to blame yourself

Tim arrived on campus as an honor student, the son of one of the top attorneys in his home state. He had high expectations, and his goal was to follow in his father's footsteps and become a leading attorney himself. He was right on track, earning a very high grade point average in high school, and even becoming the school's Valedictorian. He arrived to college as an English and Pre-law major, prepared to do extremely well in college. The first semester was a bit of a distraction for him. He found that the joys of college and the freedom were unlike anything he'd ever seen. Not having his mother around to make sure that he did his homework, he found himself studying less and less, and letting some things slide that he would normally have gotten done.

It wasn't long before Tim started to see the consequences of his actions. His grades went to levels that he never dreamed they would. Before long, he was on a downward spiral, not to return back to normal. The same way that he once had a habit of making good grades, he now found that earning bad grades was his new habit. Once he got used to getting Cs and Ds, it was difficult to earn better grades. Eventually, his dream of becoming an attorney died, as he ended up dropping out of school.

The thing I noticed about Tim's experience was that when his mother called me, baffled about her son's performance, she felt that it was her fault that he was struggling. She somehow thought that she had not raised him correctly, or that she had done something else to contribute to his demise. I explained to her that although it is tough to remember, her son is old enough to make many decisions on his own. Unless she was willing to move in with him, there was no way that she was going to keep him from making the choices he made (no, I do NOT recommend moving in with your kids!).

Many parents make the same mistake as Tim's mother. They somehow feel that they are to blame when their child does something stupid. The sad reality is that kids don't need parents to teach them to be stupid, they can usually learn to be stupid on their own. I did some pretty dumb things when I was in college, and they were completely the result of my own creativity. They had nothing to do with my mother, but she also chose to blame herself when I made mistakes. This is part of human nature. The clear moral is that our family members are sometimes going to make choices that we cannot control. That is something that we all must accept.

Have the student think about what happened and why they struggled

It is extremely important that your child become empowered by their bad academic experience. I have always believed that life gives you two sets of choices: to end the game with a basketful of excuses, or to finish with a basketful of results. Kids make excuses, we all did. The funny thing is that many times, an excuse can be perfectly valid. But the problem is that excuses don't get us where we want to go. *Life will always give you a really good reason to fail.* . It is our personal choice whether we want to accept the excuse presented to us, or if we want to get what we came for.

The first thing that many students, especially freshmen, are tempted to do is make an excuse for why they struggled academically.

"The professor is no good, he was so unfair!"
"I studied as hard as I could, and I still failed"
"My course load was too heavy and I couldn't study"

The list of excuses seems longer than life itself. Kids are good at coming up with excuses, and you can't blame them. Our first natural instinct when we enter this world is to blame others for our failures, but we all like to take credit for our successes. It is up to our parents to teach us to be responsible for our actions, no matter what they are.

When your child struggles in school, the only way that they are going to learn to do better is if a) you do not accept the poor performance, and b) you force them to think about what they did wrong. I am constantly baffled by the number of parents that sit and watch their kids come home with Cs and Ds every semester without doing anything about it. Given that you are investing in this person, they should be forced to invest their efforts as well.

The self-reflective process should not only include an examination of study strategies (i.e. "I studied for biology in the wrong way"), it should also include an analysis of the child's habits and time management ability. What time do they normally get up in the morning? How consistently do

178

they prepare for exams? How well do they plan for the semester? Questions like this should be answered as the student is forced to analyze their personal habits and factors that might have led to the poor performance.

Here are some additional questions you might have your child ask himself/herself after having a bad semester:

1) Do I go meet with my teachers regularly?
2) Who am I studying with?
3) Where do I do most of my studying?
4) What is my strategy for getting ready for a big test? Do I find myself cramming a lot?
5) When I study, do I allow for distractions in my working environment?
6) When do I tend to study well? When do I tend to study poorly? (i.e. Do I study better when I have a test coming up or when my girlfriend is out of town?)

Have your child ask and answer these questions, and you will be surprised at what kinds of insights they find in the process.

Force them to come up with a plan

Obviously, as the parent, you have some role to play in getting your child out of their funk if you choose to be part of this process. The first thing you have a right to do is force the child to come up with a plan for how they are going to work themselves out of the mess that they've created.

The plan should be one created by the child, not you. It is important that you make sure that you don't come in like Superman and take over the process. That is not your job. Your job is to help them turn this costly experience into a valuable lesson. That is not going to happen if they are not forced to think through what just happened and grow as a result of their experience.

After they come up with a plan, it would be your job to agree and approve it. You should be careful not to allow the child to give you the same old stuff as before, since that is not going to be any good in this context. That means that the plan should include something that is going to change about their behavior, something they are going to do differently. The change should not be something simple, like "I am going to study more". Instead, it should be something more concrete like "I am going to go to the library 5 days per week and stay at least 4 hours each time", or "I am not going to study in my dorm room anymore."

Demand a balanced performance

I can't tell you how many times I've heard very bright students say something like "I do really well in the classes I like, but I don't do so well in the ones that I hate." This is a cute statement in some ways, since many of us would have said the same thing when we were younger. But what we learned (hopefully) is that you can't halfway do things in life just because you don't like them. In the workforce, your boss is more likely to remember the things that you did poorly than the things you did well, so you should have *everything* in good shape if you want to be respected.

I have seen brilliant students who've done extremely well in their major, only to have their graduate school and job opportunities go out the window just because they chose to be undisciplined in the way they applied their intelligence. The student would get As in their favorite classes, and then get Ds in the ones that they hate. That has always confused me, since that person would lose the chance to do what they love in graduate school because of their low GPA.

As a parent, there are things you can do to lead your child to understand the importance of a balanced effort. First, you can make sure that you remind them of the grades that aren't so good. That might mean actually imposing some kind of penalty for these grades. Second, listen to their logic. If their excuse for doing poorly in a class is "I hated it", then you should probably explain why this class matters when it comes to their future. Also, you should explain what I just said, how not doing the things you don't enjoy can keep you from doing the things you love.

Being hard and soft at the same time

If your child has any sense of personal responsibility, there is a chance that they already feel pretty bad about their poor performance. This means that hammering things into their head may not be the way to go. Sometimes, if you say something once, they get it. Keep saying it, your voice gets translated to "blah blah blah".

It is a tough balance to know how to be supportive, yet challenging at the same time. Since you know your child best, I am going to leave that one to you. However, I would do what I could to avoid being too much of one thing or the other, since that is not the way to get people motivated.

Does your child go see the professor?

No matter how prepared your student is for college, meeting with the professor is a good way to avoid a lot of headaches. For some reason, students see the professor as some high and mighty cog in a process that dominates them. While I certainly feel that students should respect professors, they should not be afraid to see them and even confront them if necessary.

Going to see the professor is something that gives the student the best tutor on earth. The professor knows the stuff like the back of his/her hand, and most of my students find that the material is much easier once I've been able to guide them through it. But there are some things that students should realize about professors, at least professors like me.

First, professors *hate when students come to their office unprepared.* This does not mean that you have to know everything in the world about the topic. If you knew that much, you wouldn't need to come visit. What I mean is that the student needs to have at least done what they can on their end to make sure that the professor's time is not wasted teaching the student things that they could have read on their own. I can usually tell in an instant if the student sees me as someone who can get them over the hump, or as someone who is expected to carry them 8 miles just to get to the hump that they need to cross. While both of these students are going to get my help, the one expecting me to carry him/her is going to be in for a rude awakening when I tell them that I can only talk for 30 minutes.

Secondly, students need to realize that coming to meet the professor right before the exam is extremely difficult. I laugh because my office is always empty all month, until the days before the test. That is when I stand there, like the Pope forgiving the sins of those students who chose not to do the right thing when they had the chance. They line up out the door, each of them waiting for 5 minutes with me as I simply tell many of them that there is only so much I can do to help them at this late stage.

The smart student is the one that takes advantage of the periods when other students are ignoring the professor. They come see me when they are Jamming, so that they can have me all to themselves. They come into my office and get personalized help for hours on end, mainly because their classmates are still sitting at home with their Play Station videogames. These are students that professors respect, and these are the ones that are going to get the most help during the week of the exam, since they've been coming to visit the professor all along.

There are usually teaching assistants for large classes. These people can be extremely helpful, sometimes even more so than the professors. The office hours of the TA should be used up as much as possible before you consider paying more money to a tutor.

Every student should get a tutor for difficult courses. You should think of a tutor as an attorney: just get one to have on stand by in case you need him/her. You don't have to constantly pay a tutor when you don't need them, but perhaps when you start that really difficult Biology class, you go ahead and find one, instead of having to make a mad scramble for one later.

The biggest mistake that students make when it comes to tutors is that they get one when it's too late. They fail the first test, and they say "OK, if I do poorly the second time, I am going to think about getting a tutor." Then, they fail the second test. Well, many college courses don't have more than 3 exams, so by the time you've failed two exams, you are headed to hell in a hand basket. You end up scraping and working like crazy to get that D, when that same effort all semester would have gotten an easy "A".

A tutor should be obtained at the beginning of difficult courses and used as a preventative measure to secure an "A", rather than prevent an "F". They should only be paid when you have exhausted all other options: you have visited your teacher every week, gone to see the Teaching Assistant, and worked with friends in the class to see if they can help you. By the time you work with the tutor, you are already on top of your game, so you don't have to pay this person to teach you things that you could have learned for free.

When I was in college, I made A FORTUNE from students who were not prepared. They would call me in the middle of the exam week (I had already prepared for my finals, so I made sure that this week was open for business), and beg me to help them get ready for their test. Of course I was usually booked up by finals week, so I was able to write my own check. Not that my goal was to financially destroy anyone, but most of us are going to work for the highest bidder.

I loved the rich kids, who would use their parents' money to hire me for 20 hours in one week, perhaps paying me as much as $50 an hour to help them. This money was critical to my financial survival in college, and I found myself wealthier than a lot of my friends. What was most confusing to me was that many students would be so unprepared that I would spend half of that time teaching them basic concepts that they could have learned on their own.

Don't let your child be one of the people that makes a tutor rich for no good reason. I was not able to make all this money because I was smart. That is a common misperception of tutors. I was able to make the money because I was PREPARED. I would simply learn the material before my classmates, and then charge them money as they begged me to teach it to them. I did this because I had to do this to survive, since I was responsible for my own financial situation in college. So, rather than waiting for others to take care of me, my situation led me to find a personally productive way to support myself and learn my coursework all at the same time.

Ways to get a tutor if you don't have a lot of money

If you and your child cannot afford a tutor by combining your incomes, check campus resources. Many campuses have ways that you can get tutors cheap. Sometimes, you get what you pay for though. I recall my campus having a free tutoring service, but they could never get math or science tutors because the pay was too low. I would get only $8 per hour from their office, but at the same time, get offers of $20 per hour from private students. Additionally, those who took the university tutors only had help for 2 hours per week, while those who paid someone privately were unlimited.

Another option for paying for a tutor is to work as a group. Sometimes, if you negotiate properly, you can get the tutor to charge a group of say, 3 students the price that they would charge 1.5 – 2 students individually. This is a good way to save money. The important thing here, however, is to make sure that you work with a group of students of the same caliber or better. If you are working with students that either do not work hard or are always behind, your child will find themselves sitting there angry that they have to wait for the other kid to catch up.

If your child chooses to work in a group, they should be encouraged to stay with that group after the tutor is gone. That way, they can push one another to do better in the class. But the key is that they find a group to work with that also has a desire to do well in the course.

Another way to get an inexpensive tutor is for the child to find someone in the class who does extremely well. Many times, you can offer that person half of what the tutor would require, and they will do the job. They are happy to take the cash because they were not expecting to earn it in the first place. When I was a freshman, I had a rich kid offer me the chance to tutor her in the class I was taking with her. I didn't expect this, but I welcomed it. I made a lot of money, and her grade rose from an "F" to a "B". We both walked away satisfied.

The best and cheapest tutors on campus are the professors and the Teaching Assistants. It makes no sense to pay a private tutor right off the bat if the student is not going to see the teacher. Professors are not high and mighty Greek Gods that the students should be afraid of.

186

They are regular people who sit around wondering why students don't come to see them. Tell your child that they should visit their professor and T.A.s every week, even if there is no homework due.

Repeating classes

One of the things that many universities allow students to do is repeat classes in which they've had a poor performance. The nice catch to this is that there may even be the opportunity to *repeat the class and not have it factored into the student's GPA.* That is the benefit of repeating a class. Learning the subject is, honestly, a distant second.

I personally used repeat options 3 times during my college career. I had 3 grades that I was not so proud of, and after retaking these courses, my GPA improved quite a bit. The impact of repeat options is two fold: first, you are getting rid of one of your worst grades, and secondly, you are gaining one of your best. Well, that is if you do it right.

To give you an example, consider the following:

A student has taken 45 credit hours (with all classes having the same number of credits) and has a 2.5 GPA. Their lowest 3 grades are two Ds and an F. The student chooses to retake their classes and earns As in all 3 of them. Their GPA would go from 2.5 to 3.25.

The math for the above problem is slightly complicated, but can be understood in the following way: A grade point average comes from the total number of "quality points" that a student has, divided by the number of credit hours:

$$GPA = \frac{\text{Quality Points}}{\text{Credit Hours}}$$

The key to making the GPA high is to make sure that the top of this fraction is high in comparison to the bottom. Let's say that you take away the child's worst 3 classes. That means that the top is going to change, but not by very much. For example, you get no quality points for an F, so getting rid of 3 Fs is not going to change the top at all. But the bottom is going to change, since the number of credit hours earned is going to drop when you take classes away. The fact that the bottom is smaller, while the top remains the same means that the whole fraction is going to get a lot bigger (kind of like having the same size cake to share with fewer kids).

Now, let's say that you repeat those 3 classes and do very well. The bottom is going to go up again, since the credit hours earned is going to increase, but the top goes up even more, since each good grade gives the student lots of quality points. So, this would be like getting 3 more kids, but getting a lot of cake to feed the extra kids at the birthday party. The point is that the top of the fraction has been increased a great deal, and the bottom hasn't been changed very much at all.

You should encourage your child to use as many repeat options as they can as they move forward with college. Retaking a class can be painful, but it can also be rewarding. When choosing a class to retake, I recommend that the student retake something concrete, like Math or Science. Retaking something like English can be risky, since much of your grade can be based on the subjectivity of the professor.

Academic Bankruptcy

Most universities have an escape mechanism for those students with serious academic problems. This process is called "academic bankruptcy" at some schools, but nearly every college has something like it. This process is the same as standard bankruptcy, in which the student gets the chance to start off with a clean slate, but only with certain conditions. The conditions might vary from one school to the next, but they are usually quite challenging for the student and their family.

The hardest part about this process is that it can be expensive. I have seen universities that will allow a student to begin college fresh, but they are forced to pay tuition all over again for the classes they retake. This leads to an entire year of wasted money, time and effort.

Your child should consider academic bankruptcy if their grade point average is horribly low. Arbitrarily, I consider anything below a 2.0 after the Freshman year to be a good cutoff. However, I have seen students declare bankruptcy with higher GPAs, perhaps if they wanted to go to medical school or something later. Also, if there are extraordinary circumstances surrounding the poor performance, the student may declare bankruptcy for that as well. If this is the case with your child, you should take the issue up with the academic administrators. Make sure that your child is part of the process, since they should also be involved.

Academic bankruptcy might mean a clean slate, but it's not completely clean. Some would say that it's just not as dirty as the old one. When your child retakes their courses (and this is also true with repeat options), the transcript still tells the entire story. That means that many universities will put something on the transcript that states that although the original GPA is not factored in, the student did repeat the classes in which they performed poorly. It is only fair that universities have this rule, since it is not fair to give bankrupt students the same academic accolades as those who did everything right the first time. In some ways it is also sad. I have seen students denied the right to become Summa Cum Laude because they had declared bankruptcy early in their academic career.

Do not allow your child to put himself/herself in this position. An ounce of prevention is certainly worth a pound of cure. While these things certainly happen and can be managed, it makes more sense to do the work early on to avoid these problems.

Following the Crowd

"They dared me to do it, so I just jumped." – College student, explaining why he jumped off a 250 foot high bridge and nearly drowned.

If your child is human, they are probably affected by peer pressure. The group of peers may change, but the outcome remains the same. This is a sad and challenging part of dealing with kids and raising them. We all go through it, both as parents and as people. Even when we are in our 30s, 40s and 50s, we find ourselves paying attention to what our peers think of us.

The difference seems to be that when you are older, you know that following your peers is the quickest way to end up in a bad situation. Kids don't know this yet, especially college students. What I also find is that the students who are least secure about their identity are the ones that are most likely to fall victim to the pitfalls of peer pressure. The group mentality of students can lead to the insane drunken riots that take place after football championships, and the deaths and injuries that occur at fraternity and sorority parties. The problems can be quite serious and you do not want your child to be a victim of these tragic circumstances. The story I am about to tell you is flat out disgusting, but true. I am going to risk the consequences of sharing this story in hopes that it will give you some idea of how strong the peer pressure can be:

Billy was trying hard to join the fraternity. He wanted badly to be part of the same group his father belonged to, so he was willing to do whatever it took. Unfortunately for Billy, the leaders in the fraternity were not using their power responsibly. Rather than giving them tasks that were simply meant to scare them psychologically, they gave them tasks that were physically and mentally damaging.

On this night, Billy was told, along with 3 other fraternity "pledges" to take off his pants and get on his knees. Between the three of them was a big cookie cake, about 18 inches in diameter. The men were then told to masturbate. They were told to masturbate in such a way that the semen would land on the cookie cake. As if this assignment were not shocking enough, the last part shocked him most. The last person to have an orgasm on the cookie cake was the one that would be forced to eat it. Billy's fraternity brothers kept their promise and forced him to eat the entire thing. This event scarred him for life.

Again, I apologize for telling a story that could be offensive to some and definitely disgusting to others. But this lets you know that peer pressure can lead your child to do things that are psychologically damaging or extremely hurtful. I have never quite understood what makes students do the things they do, but I do know that they are willing to do them. I have some thoughts on how you can prepare your child for this kind of environment. You may want to share these tips with them during a conversation.

Have your child read a book about college before they arrive

Your child should be made aware of everything that goes on inside and outside the classroom long before they get to campus. It is up to you to put something in front of them that describes the college process in brutally honest detail. You may also want to tell them to write a book report and submit it to you. This common sense can be extremely helpful when your child heads to campus.

By reading about the things that happen on campus before they confront them, students are more likely to feel empowered in their new environment, rather than controlled by it. Make sure that they get what they need.

Teach them the power of independent thinking

It is my experience that the child that is most secure in their identity and best able to think independently is the one that is least likely to be affected by peer pressure. The first thing you want your child to know is that just because something happens in college, that doesn't make it right. It is important that your child understand this early, for many students feel that there is security in large numbers.

One of the benefits I felt in college was the fact that although I was shy, I knew stupidity when I saw it. It didn't matter that everyone in the room was doing something, I would just know that it wasn't something I was supposed to be doing. You want your child to have that same level of understanding. Not only will they be able to identify unhealthy behavior, they will have the courage to reject it.

It may be tough to teach a child to think independently. The best you can do as a parent is simply explain to them that they should be proud of who they are, no matter what. They should never let anyone make them feel bad for who they are. You may also want to tell your own stories about how people you grew up with and followed around ended up in bad situations. This will help them draw the link between you and their own friends, and they will most likely come to the right conclusions.

194

Let them feel the burn from their mistakes

This point cannot be emphasized enough. Another deterrent to following the crowd are the consequences. If parents shelter their kids from consequences of the choices they make, then the child is never going to learn from their mistakes. There are times when you might want to be there for some degree of security, but ultimately, you want to "let them hit their head" a few times if that is what it takes to get them to make the right choices. This will make them think twice before doing things that might be hurtful to their future.

I've been around students for many years. They are smarter than you think. If you are going to be there to save them every time they make a mistake, they know it. I've heard some really interesting conversations by students, the ones where the kid says "Yeah, I got arrested, but it was cool, my dad took care of it. When's the next party dude?" The problem with the "mom and dad will protect me" logic is that there may come a time when you can't save them. If they are coddled time after time, they will do things that are worse and worse until they finally do something that is so bad that you can't save them no matter what you do.

Bob was a straight A student, and a Senior. He was planning to be a Veterinarian one day, since that had been his lifelong dream. One night, he was out with friends drinking. The students made the mistake of going out without a designated driver, and since all of them were pretty "toasted", no one had the good sense to realize that there was no one fit to get behind the wheel. Bob was the one who chose to drive, and out of the 4 that got into the car, he was the only one that emerged from it. All 3 of his friends died that night, along with two drivers in the car going in the opposite direction.

Now Bob, the straight A student, was facing serious prison time. His parents were affluent, but when your child is responsible for killing 5 people, even the best attorneys can't do much. Bob spent 5 years in prison and was released for good behavior. As a felon, he is not able to attend many graduate schools. As he rebuilds his life, he now spends his time visiting college campuses and speaking to kids about the dangers of driving drunk.

Be able to forgive, don't nag

As much as we might want to choke our children for mistakes they make, we have to remember that we all make mistakes. This is a part of learning and growing up. So, when you get that call in the middle of the night, try to control your emotions as much as possible. The goal as a parent is to teach, and remember that there is a trade off: if fighting through these consequences is enough to keep the child from ever making the mistake again, then typically, the mistake as a good thing, not a bad one.

Summers: What Should your Kids Be Doing With Them?

"I was able to beat the 'Halo' videogame on the hardest level. It took 10 hours a day, but I did it." – College student, after being asked what he did with his summer.

In my books *Everything You Ever Wanted to Know about College – A Guide for Minority Students* and *Quick and Dirty Secrets of College Success*, I talk extensively about what students should do with their summers. I do this because, in my experience, students and their parents have a lot of trouble figuring out what to do with their kids when school is out.

This problem baffles and shocks me, all at the same time. We seem to have another problem in our culture: this image of the student going off to a tough year of college, and then coming home with a car full of "stuff" every May, hanging out and doing nothing all summer long. During this time, they make friends, have romances, and get fat. Perhaps if they feel up to it, they might go work in a grocery store. To be quite honest, these images really make me sick!

Summers are not supposed to be wasted. 25% of the time that your child spends in college is going to be summer. Do you really want them to waste that much time? Let me tell you a story that illustrates my point:

John was a good student, with a grade point average that was above 3.0 on a 4.0 scale. He was a Marketing major and had plans to get a job with an Advertising agency upon graduation. He was a smart, ambitious student, but one who did not use his summers for productive activity. It wasn't that he was a bad or lazy kid, he just didn't know what the competition was doing.

Upon graduation, John had earned a 3.6 grade point average, which was highly competitive relative to his peers. But he was shocked when interviewing with companies, who seemed relatively unimpressed with his grades. The first question he usually heard was "Do you have any work experience?" His answer of "Not really, but I'm trying right now" didn't seem to impress his employers very much.

You can imagine how disappointed John's parents were when they saw him using his Marketing Degree selling shoes for slightly above minimum wage after graduation. This was hardly the life that John had planned for himself, and not the life on which his parents wanted to spend $80,000 in tuition money.

One of the biggest mistakes that college students make is that of work experience. They forget that companies don't usually want to hire someone that has no experience. Those companies that have their choice of the best students are going to choose the student with good grades AND work experience over those that have just one or the other. So, if you do not encourage your child to use their summers to reach this goal, they are going to be at a disadvantage.

Working is not the only productive thing that students can do with their summers. In order of my personal ranking, I list the things that I think your child should be doing in the summer:

1) Getting work experience

Since your goal is to make sure that your child is gainfully employed upon graduation, I recommend that you make sure that those issuing employment will find your child employable! Work experience is the best way to do this, particularly if your child has a major in which work experience is critical. There are some majors in which this is not true, perhaps Philosophy or English. But if your child majors in business, engineering or anything in which they would like a job after graduation, they should get all the work experience they can get.

Additionally, the students who get work experience via internships have the inside track when it comes to hiring opportunities. I have seen students with lower GPAs win favor over students with higher GPAs when the high GPA students had not spent their time networking. Unfortunately, we all know that in this world, what you know is always a distant second to who you know.

2) Study abroad programs

I remember once talking to an employer who said the following to me "Boyce, the students who have spent time overseas are not looked at the same as those who have stayed in the U.S." That was enough for me to recommend to many of my students that they do something out of the country before they leave college. Study abroad programs are one way to do this, and many universities have these programs available.

A preferred approach might be for the student to find an overseas internship, so that they can make money and spend time out of the country. However, the difficulty in obtaining this kind of opportunity can vary from one university to the next. I recommend that if you want your child to gain something that is going to be of value to them for the rest of their life, you should send them overseas for a summer.

3) **Summer School**

If your child is unable to obtain an internship or study abroad opportunity, the next best thing for them to consider would be summer school. When I was in college, I did 3 summers of summer school and one summer on an internship in Boston. Summer school was great for several reasons. First, I was able to get a lot of credit hours out of the way, which gave me the option of graduating early. I chose not to, but I could have if I had wanted. Secondly, it gave me the chance to have fun and be productive, all at the same time. Third, a really difficult class is not going to be as difficult during the summer as it is during the rest of the year. So, your child might be able to get that scary math class out of the way during the summer, rather than taking it in the fall when it is even scarier.

Unbeknownst to me at that time, there was an added benefit of going to summer school. Being at school reduced the chances that I would go home and get into trouble. I had a few friends who were not doing the right things with their lives, and the fact that I was away at college gave me a chance to grow apart from them and to steer clear from the problems they were creating in their lives. This might be relevant for your child as well.

4) **At least make sure that they get a job**

If your child has absolutely no options whatsoever during the summer, at least make sure that they get a job. Don't let them sit around at home doing nothing, for that is not how the real world works. Sitting around and being lazy is not going to help them in the long run or the short run, since they are going to arrive back at school just as lazy as they were during the summer.

If your child is home, try to convince them to find a job that they can put on their resume, even if it's volunteer work. An empty resume at graduation is the easiest way to keep an empty bank account. You should also make sure that they are working full time, not just a few hours a week. This is important for building their work ethic as they come back to campus the following year. I say this because the worst thing in the world for a professor is to see a student that is no more disciplined when they leave campus than they were when they arrived.

Things that your Daughters Need to Know

"I just woke up and saw that he was having sex with me." –
College rape victim.

Women and men have different college experiences and different problems. While it is not my goal to generalize, I can mention some things that females need to hear before they head to a college campus. It is important that you, as the parent, share this information with her and let her know how she can be best prepared to get the most out of her future and to avoid mistakes.

If she is out on a date with a guy that she hardly knows, get her to take a friend with her

The first piece of information is needed for an obvious reason. The dating game in college is a lot different from that of high school. Your daughter is suddenly faced with many guys that are a lot older than her, more experienced, more conniving and more demanding. The age of guys on campuses can go as high as 40, with many of them being in their mid 20s. The idea of your 18-year old daughter dating guys that old can be quite frightening.

Another unfortunate reality is that date rape is especially common on college campuses. More than 90% of all campus rapes occur with a familiar acquaintance. Also, between 12 and 20% of all college women are raped at some point during their college careers[vi]. What is most interesting is that the guys who do this kind of thing are "nice guys", the kinds of guys that most 18-year old girls would trust completely.

Your daughter can protect herself best by making sure that she has someone else there with her. Eventually, she may spend time alone with the guy, but perhaps by then,

204

she will have a better idea if she can trust him. Although nothing is guaranteed, there are precautions she can take to avoid some problems early on.

If she chooses to drink, tell her that she should not drink anything that she did not make herself or watch someone else make in public

There is a drug on campuses called Rohypnol. It's also known as "roofies", "roaches", "rope", "r2", etc. The drug basically makes the person who takes it feel dizzy, pass out and suffer from amnesia. Many rape victims have unknowingly taken this drug, which is why it is used by some perpetrators.

Your child may be made aware of Rohypnol at some point, but you should give her advanced warning. The conventional wisdom is that a person should not drink anything that has been out of their sight, even for one second. Additionally, if your child feels that she has been a victim of this drug, she should contact the police and go to the hospital for testing. You can be tested for the drug within the next 48 hours.

When she goes out at night, she should not walk across campus alone

Many campuses stay pretty well lit, but there are places that "bad guys" can hide pretty well. If your daughter likes to study at night, she should find a buddy to walk to the library with her.

In general, all students should not go out at night, since a great deal of crime around campuses is not reported. There are many prestigious universities placed near very bad neighborhoods. Students can be lulled into a sense of complacency on campus, and this complacency should be held under control.

When I taught at a large state university in the Midwest, I recall seeing the news about a guy and girl coming home from a party, walking by some railroad tracks. The tracks were generally safe, but what the students did not know was that there was a killer on the loose, a man who had traveled the railroads of the US killing unsuspecting victims. The male student was killed that night, and his girlfriend was raped. Their lives were never the same.

College guys can be liars sometimes

Freshmen are really naïve and trusting when they get to campus. That is why there is usually a long line of junior and senior guys waiting to lie to them. Simply letting your daughter know this in advance might help her to avoid some hard lessons.

Many times, girls can find out what a guy is all about by asking older women on campus if they know of him. Many of the biggest hounds already have a reputation that precedes them, and this reputation information may come in handy. Additionally, as much as your daughter might be excited about her newfound freedom, encouraging her to slow down with the opposite sex might actually work. But then again, did that ever stop any of us?

Tell her where the rape counseling and Planned Parenthood Offices are

Unfortunately, your child may not share all of her experiences with you. Do your best to leave the channels of communication open. At the same time, encourage her to involve the authorities when things happen to her on campus. Many young girls on campus go through the most horrible experiences, and tell no one about them.

There was a young woman on campus with an incredibly abusive boyfriend. Her parents were not involved with her, and she felt that this older guy was a protective force in her life. Perhaps he really did love her, but he showed it in very strange ways. I recall one night in particular, when the girl would go into the guy's room, and then emerge with fresh blood coming out of her nose or through her skin. She would then go back into the room and come out with even more bruises. After witnessing this process about 6 times over, we eventually figured out that the guy had been drinking and seemed to feel that he should take it out on his young girlfriend. Eventually, she came out of the room for good, with so much blood coming from her face that she left a trail on the floor. We felt bad for her and were afraid.

Noticing that the Freshman girl was too afraid to do anything, we called the police. When the officer arrived, the woman denied everything. As the officer was about to walk out the door, I called him back and told him everything I had seen. I was only a college sophomore at the time, but I knew that it was wrong for this girl to go through this, even if she did not know it. The man was eventually arrested, and the girl was very angry at me for telling the officer what I saw. But the good news is that she received some hint of the protection that she needed.

I remember not understanding why this girl allowed her boyfriend to beat her up so much. At the same time, I do understand that she was young and he was older. Also, she wasn't getting much support from home, so she didn't feel that there was anyone with whom she could share her challenges. I feel bad for this girl, for she probably married this jerk, and I am sure her life is miserable for it.

Keep your own condoms, never take it off

This last piece of advice is a mix of information that basically teaches your daughter that she should arrive on campus empowered when it comes to her life and her sexuality. That means that there is nothing wrong with carrying a condom or two, even if there are some stupid enough to call her bad names for doing so. The reality is that she should have her own protection, since she does not want to leave this in the control of someone else. I have heard of guys keeping old condoms or breaking them during sex, which is a scary thing. Your daughter should be prepared for this.

Taking the condom off is something that some college students do. Usually, this decision is driven by one of those conversations in which the students feel that they are more mature than they really are. Without realizing how incredibly dumb this decision is, they say something like "We had a talk about it, and we decided to have sex without condoms." This might be when the girl has no idea who else the guy is sleeping with, or the guy thinks that the girl is someone that she is not. It's all silly, we know that. But your daughter does not. You should explain to your child that taking the condom off is only something that is done after marriage, and only if you trust your husband completely.

What You Should Tell Your Son

"They were making fun of our fraternity, so I just stabbed his ass" – Fraternity member, after being arrested for murder.

When it comes to men, our testosterone can get us into all kinds of trouble. This is especially true for young men on campus, who have not yet learned to control the emotions that ride within them. There is nothing like being an 18-year old that is angry, jumpy and horny all at the same time. But there have been many males who've found themselves in serious trouble after one wild night that got out of control. While some of these issues are universal for males and females, I am going to address them for your male child. These are the pitfalls I've witnessed most during my time on campus, as a professor and student. These are also the issues that you should discuss with your male child.

Promiscuity is a good way to end up in some bad situations

John was a bit of a "playa". He usually had a new woman every week and he prided himself on that fact. He was certainly the envy of his friends. So while John might have been a liar, he was certainly not a rapist. "I can get it without even asking sometimes, there is no way that I'm gonna take it!" he would brag to his friends.

John worked in a local fast food restaurant, and one of the new employees would certainly be his latest "conquest". He put the smooth moves on her, and before long, she was his like the rest. John took the girl to his house and had a wonderful night of sex with her. After that night was over, he then decided to move on to the next woman.

But apparently, the girl had other plans. She had sex with John believing that he actually cared for her and wanted to be with her for good. An angry argument took place the following day after work, and like the rest of his trash, he dismissed her to be alone with her tears.

The next day, as John got ready for work, there was a knock at the door. He was greeted by a police officer, who quickly put him in handcuffs and carried him away. To his surprise, he was charged with rape.

Fortunately for John, he had money saved, about $3,500. He was going to use the money for his new car, but instead, that money now lies in the coffers of a local attorney. He was forced to drop out of school for the semester, for it is tough to study when you have to spend a week in jail. He was also fortunate enough to have the charges dropped, since it turned out that this woman had made false rape charges against several others in the past, usually suing the restaurant she worked for and settling out of court. Apparently, it was John that was the victim, and this girl was more than a pretty face.

This story is not uncommon. Mistakes like this have destroyed the lives of many young men who had no idea that there were those who could be so vindictive. What is also sad is that these men are, many times, those who have played with the hearts of the women that have trusted them so much. This does not, in any way, justify the revenge. But if you hurt someone who has the power to destroy you, you should not be surprised if they do.

The best thing to tell your son is to respect his body. There is nothing wrong with sex, in my opinion. But the sex should be meaningful, not something where you end the night asking "What is your last name again?" Promiscuity is one of the biggest issues that male students run into and are tempted by the most.

Getting into bed with a woman you barely know is dangerous for many reasons. First, you have no idea what is going on inside the woman. You could be making your own version of the movie "Fatal Attraction". Second, you could get her pregnant and end up spending your life dealing with an extremely difficult person. It must be horrible to have your kids raised by a woman with whom you have little common ground. Third, the more people you have sex with, the more likely you are to catch a very bad venereal disease.

No means no!

I can't tell you how many times I've seen guys who really believe that if a woman says "No", she might mean "yes". The question we have to ask ourselves is "Why would they believe such a thing?" I think that there is logic in this belief. If you watch movies that describe the romantic process, you usually see some guy chasing the woman until her legs fall off. Eventually, the guy wins her over, and he has her heart forever. Many would also expect the sexual process to go the same way, and in many cases, it actually does.

The problem with this is that while a high percentage of women might say "no" when they really mean "yes", there is a higher percentage that say "no" when they really mean "no". The fact that one is not able to distinguish between who says "no" and really means it and those who are just pretending says that they should not take that chance.

The stakes are too high. Rape sentences are long and the label of a sex offender is certainly not one that your child should have to carry if they did nothing to deserve it. What is sad is that this can come from one quick mistake, or even a lie from someone who simply wants to be hurtful. This is a lot of power for someone else to have, and it's up to your son to make sure that he knows this and protects himself.

Your son probably needs to understand that even if he is in the middle of sexual intercourse with a woman, if she says "stop", he needs to stop right away. Continuing from that point on technically constitutes rape. Also, it should be explained to him that a real woman will tell you that they want sex when they actually want it. A girl that plays games is just that....a girl playing games. If the girl is angered that your son has walked away during sex because she said "no", then he should explain to her that she should say what she means.

The final point is that sex and alcohol should not be mixed. This can lead to bad judgment on the part of both parties. Tell your child that when it comes to making sexual decisions, they should make them without the influence of alcohol and/or drugs.

Always carry condoms and never take them off

This is the same advice I gave the women, since we should all use condoms when having sex with someone to whom we are not married. Male hormones can be a very strong thing (females too). If someone is not prepared, they may or may not have the discipline to wait until they have protection. Your son should be prepared for all occasions.

Avoid violence at all costs

One of the things that I've noticed about many young men starting college is that they forget they are over the age of 18. They don't realize that once you are 18, fighting someone does not have the same meaning as it did when you were a kid. When you are an adult, fighting constitutes assault, for which you can be arrested.

As silly as it may sound, you have to explain this to your son. At the same time, you have to create some sort of non-violent resolution to the problems your son is likely to face on a college campus. Pride is important to a man, and he may be happier having a way to resolve disputes without losing his dignity in the process. Sometimes it might be just walking away. Other times, it might be letting campus authorities know what is going on. If your son is dealing with the threat of physical violence and no one is responding to him, then perhaps you should become involved and let the university know.

When I was a freshman in college, I had the roommate from hell. This guy loved to drink, and he was an absolute jerk. He would come into the room at 3 AM on a school night and slam the door repeatedly, even though he knew that we both had class the following day. To be honest, I despised him.

One night, I'd had enough. He had spit his chewing tobacco onto a nice suit that I owned, and I was furious! It

216

seemed as though no one cared what I was going through, since the issue had been ignored by my dorm monitor. So, after losing my patience, I was going to wait until my roommate arrived to the room and beat him into the ground. But fortunately, my mother talked sense into me. She convinced me to go to the Head of Residence Life, who helped me in getting the jerk out of my room. I was successful, more so than I would have been had I taken the law into my own hands.

My experience is quite common on campus. What was interesting was that I had no idea how much trouble I would have gotten into had I gotten into a fight with my roommate. You would be amazed at how little students understand about these things.

I knew of a student at a well-respected university who had a problem with homosexuals. He was a very good student, but his hatred of gays eventually lead to his downfall. Apparently, one of the men his dorm was gay and he seemed to enjoy flirting with this student, not knowing about his homophobia. One day when the student had enough, he proceeded to beat the gay man with a baseball bat until he had brain damage. The student received several years in prison for what he had done. Make sure that your child is aware.

Choose the right guys to run around with

Many times, it's not enough to do the right thing your self. We also need to avoid being around those who do not do the right thing. I have seen just as many guys get into lots of trouble for being around others doing the wrong thing as I have seen guys get into trouble for what they themselves have done.

When your son goes to college, encourage him to choose his friends wisely. If he joins a fraternity, tell him to join one that focuses on the values that he deems important, not just the guys that seem the coolest at the time. These are going to be his peers in college, and the ones who influence him the most. Being around the right people can make all the difference.

What if Your Child Wants to Move Off Campus?

"I figured that it would be cheaper living off campus, but now I wish I was back in the dorm." – College Senior after moving into her own apartment.

Moving off campus is an interesting rite of passage for many students. For some, this is the point where they go from childhood to adulthood. It is the first time they have bills to pay, and even more freedom is afforded to them than they had when on campus. At least the dorms had rules and curfews, but living off campus has none of that. It can be an enlivening and exciting opportunity for students to grow up and learn how the world really works.

There are pros and cons to moving off campus. The pros are that it can be cheaper, since some universities really rip off students when it comes to housing. They provide the convenience of having everything paid for and taken care of all at once, but what they charge is usually more than what the services are worth. Many parents don't care, since they enjoy the security and simplicity of their child being on campus. I don't blame them one bit.

Living off campus also gives the student a chance to know what it's like to pay their own bills and live their own lives. This is a nice stepping-stone toward preparing the student for the world that awaits them after college. I got my first off campus apartment during my junior year. It was a good time for me to move forward, since I had out grown my dorm. At the same time, I found that living off campus was a bit lonely, since I was away from my friends and my girlfriend. In fact, my girlfriend stopped coming to visit me! I asked her why she wasn't coming to my house anymore, and she said "You live too far away." Talk about the fragility of college relationships! I guess I was a better boyfriend when I lived across the street.

The cons of living off campus can be more numerous than the pros, but that doesn't mean that the student shouldn't do it. Rather, it means that the student should beware of these issues in advance and do what they can to manage them. They are going to have to live off campus at some point in their lives, so they might as well start learning the process while they are in the latter stages of their college careers.

Con #1: Isolation

The first downside of living off campus is the detachment that the student may feel from the rest of the campus community. This is not something that most young students are aware of, since they have not gone through it before. But the fact is that when you live off campus, you end up emotionally and physically detached, which can be a dangerous thing. The emotional side is simple and obvious. I have seen students get lonely when moving off campus, to the point of being depressed. The physical detachment can be problematic for a different reason. "Out of sight, out of mind" comes to pass in this scenario, since being 10 miles from campus makes it much easier to skip out on that boring lecture that you don't want to attend anyway. This is especially tempting when you consider the bad weather and difficult campus parking. The old convenience of walking to your classes may now be gone for good.

Con #2: No one is going to manage your bills for you anymore

The second con is that your child may not be mature enough to manage themselves off campus. Living off campus involves an entirely new set of financial obligations that are going to require the student to manage their money and be responsible. Many kids are not ready for this. While the cost of living may be lower, it also has to be paid every month instead of every semester. So, it is easy to spend money that you are going to need later, and find yourself staring down the barrel of an eviction notice.

Making sure that your child is prepared

How do you best prepare your child for living off campus? First, there is no reason I can think of that a student should live off campus earlier than their Junior year. Moving off campus as a Freshman or Sophomore is, in my opinion, far too early. The student should get the chance to live life as a pure college student for at least two years, given that there are already a great many adjustments they are forced to make.

Second, if your child moves off campus, you may want to encourage them to get an apartment close to the university. In fact, the student should be able to walk to class if necessary. This is important, since the ease with which the student can get to class determines how likely they are to attend class everyday. Also, if their car breaks down, they will have the ability to make it to class, even if they have no money in their pocket.

Have a talk with your child about money management. Outline the expenses that a typical apartment renter pays every month and prepare them mentally to deal with them. Teach them to balance a checkbook and to budget their money. They may not take these lessons to heart, but at least you can say that you warned them in advance.

If your child doesn't take the advice that you give them and they find themselves in serious financial trouble, be hesitant to bail them out. This is their first chance to learn the lessons that many of us learn: if you don't manage your money, you don't get to eat or have a place to live. Don't let them get evicted (if you can avoid it), but you should give them a very hard time about it.

Talk to your child about their process in choosing a roommate. I have a story to tell:

Cynthia was excited about moving into an apartment with her two best friends, Amber and Dana. She was now a junior, so it was time for her to move off campus. At first, things were fine. The girls got along really well, and she also found herself saving money. However, things eventually turned negative, and the experience became a complete nightmare.

The first nightmare occurred when Cynthia realized the challenges of living with Dana. She had no idea that she would be living with Dana AND her disgusting boyfriend. At first, her boyfriend would come visit occasionally. Eventually, he would be there more than she was. She would find herself having to cover up to take a shower, since she had no idea if he was going to meet her in the hallway.

The second nightmare occurred when Amber ran into money problems and decided to move in the middle of the month. Of course, the remaining two roommates explained to Amber how it was too late to find a replacement and the other two girls did not have the money to pay for the apartment themselves. But this was of no consequence to Amber, since she knew the lease and all the bills were in

Cynthia's name. Cynthia had not planned on this happening, so she had no problem signing the lease while the other girls were in class. Her choice eventually came back to haunt her.

The final nightmare occurred when Amber took the liberty of making $300 in long distance phone calls right before moving out. Of course, the phone company did not care who made the calls. They only knew that the phone bill was in Cynthia's name. Cynthia, now a 27 year old, still has the negative marks on her credit that came as a result of her experience with the two roommates from hell.

Kids can do some of the silliest things sometimes when it comes to their friends and living together. They will sign for nearly anything, let their friends borrow their car, and lend large sums of money to their significant other. This is not new, since many of us made the same mistakes at their age. You should do your best to have a talk with your child about who is signing for what, to make sure that he/she does not take a disproportionate amount of the responsibility. Our kids, in their trustfulness, can sometimes make devastating financial mistakes.

The last thing that you and your child should know about moving off campus is that many universities have limited dorm space. This means that typically, when you move off campus, you cannot get back on. So, make sure that your child understands this and is emotionally prepared for the challenges and new freedoms of living on their own!

That Good Ol Fashioned Collegiate Drama – Dealing with Emotional Crises

"I just can't live without her."- The last statement made by a student on his mother's answering machine before he killed himself.

Your child will, almost without question, go through some kind of major emotional issue when they get to college. Most of the crises involve that guy or girl that they swore was going to love them forever, but was surprisingly seen kissing their best friend in the dorm lobby. It happens, you deal with it, you move on. The problem with these crises is that the highly emotional youth of college tend to go into shut down mode when bad things happen to them: they don't study, they don't eat, they do things that are self-destructive. This is natural, but still problematic.

Your role as the parent can be critical when it comes to helping your child get through these situations. I have some tips and advice on how you might want to deal with these situations as they arise. The problems might not seem important to you, but they are important to them. You don't want these issues to affect the child's academic performance.

Be there for them as much as you can

I remember calling my mother at 2 am, on a work night, on two separate occasions during college. Both calls were because of a woman. I appreciated the fact that even though my mother had to get up and go to work the next morning, she stayed up with me on the phone. I will never forget the support she showed me at such a difficult time in my life. Then, there was another time when I felt bad about the same girl that I had spent an hour or two moaning over two weeks earlier. This time, my mother told me to grow up and deal with it. That was a harsh reaction to receive from her, but you know what? I grew up and dealt with it.

226

Your child may come to you for emotional support. It is wonderful that you provide it for them, but you should not find yourself being an emotional crutch that the child can use to cry on every time something goes wrong. That is not your role. Your role is to be there when things get tough, but to know when to back away and let them fight their own battles.

Don't panic and let it ride itself out

The other thing you should know about college emotional "crises" is that they are typically temporary. A parent that panics every time their child acts as though something is bothering them will surely drive him/herself crazy.

These emotional ups and downs are part of growing up. I have seen parents that behave as though they are their child's best friend, being there for them like a roommate or buddy. I am not sure if this is the healthiest kind of relationship to have. Many students have a difficult time developing relationships with the opposite sex when that person they are attempting to relate to already has a boyfriend/girlfriend disguised as a parent. In fact, I have seen women have horrible relationships with boys who were simply looking for another mother, and men who can't have an adult relationship because their girlfriend's mother or father is too deeply involved with their child's life. There are ways to be there for your child while giving them space. If you do not, it may stunt their relationship growth and leave them seeking a mate well into their 30s.

Remind them where their rocks are

Students, like the teenagers they once were, are not going to let you in on everything that goes on in their lives. At the same time, it is important that they know where their emotional rocks lie. A student can be easily fooled into thinking that their friends or their mate love them as much as their family. Usually, these situations end in disappointment, when they find out time and again that there is no replacement for the love of family.

Let them know that you are there for them and that they can receive love from you when they are being loved by no one else. Also, you may want to fill them with good old-fashioned wisdom every now and then. They may not appear to be listening, but usually they are.

If it's too serious, encourage counseling

Most college campuses have counselors on staff to help your child work through their emotional issues. The counselors are typically as good as the expensive ones in the "real world", but they don't cost as much. Students can see the counselors for issues ranging from depression to domestic violence to couples counseling. Your child should be made aware of these resources.

If you are worried about your child and their current emotional state, talk to them about seeing a counselor. Also, talk to the resident advisor in your child's dorm, who can then keep an eye on them. A good resident advisor has been taught how to manage and deal with student issues as they arise.

Teach Your Child the Value of Their Opportunities

"It was easy to drop out of school, but it was pretty damn hard to get back in." – 28-year old college graduate, who left school for 6 years before coming back and finishing.

One of the biggest problems of college students is that many of them do not realize the value of their opportunities until those opportunities no longer exist. It is up to us to help them learn the value of these opportunities before they let them waste away.

I have some ideas on how you can make your child see the value of a college education. Perhaps trying these approaches will wake your child up to the value of their opportunities:

Show them the output

I had a friend that wanted his son to understand the value of his privileged background. In order to make the message clear, he took his son on a tour of the city. During this tour, he took his son to the worst parts of town: the local jail, the dirty streets, the places with prostitutes, the homeless, etc. What made things even more interesting was when he was able to point out to his son that the homeless guy they saw on the street used to be the captain of his high school football team. He had his son ask the homeless man what he would change if he could, and the guy said that he would have taken advantage of all of his educational opportunities. He'd had the chance to go to college on a football scholarship, but he passed it over, and ended up with a tail-spun life that included drugs, crime and unemployment. He was truly remorseful for the choices he had made.

On the second part of the tour, he took his son to the more affluent parts of town: the places with big houses, pretty neighborhoods, and nice schools. The son was impressed with this part of the city, and after seeing the worst parts, there was a tremendous contrast in his mind.

After the tour was over, my friend told his son "You have a choice. You can live either one of these lives, and I am not going to tell you which one to choose. It's completely up to you."

Now, of course this was a highly rigged tour of the city. My friend knew where his old friend from the football team would be that day, so he made sure that he "accidentally" ran into him on the street. That way, he would be able to spend the entire drive telling his son how great the guy *used* to be, how he was the coolest, the fastest and the smartest. It was his life choices that led him down the wrong path.

But my friend's strategy was impressive because it got the point across. He didn't have to tell his son to make the right choices, his son made the choices on his own. That is the key to motivation. It must come from inside, or it doesn't work. Parents who attempt to keep their kids motivated without expecting anything from the child are usually pretty exhausted in the end.

Let them meet a "Halfling"

What is a "Halfling"? That is someone who *almost* graduated from college, or perhaps they went to college for a year and then dropped out. There are many more Halflings than there are college graduates. The sad thing about this world is that no one is going to respect you because you have 60% of a college degree. It's an "in" or "out" thing, either you graduated, or you didn't. Halflings are important people for your child to meet, since hearing their reasons for dropping out are incredibly valuable information for the child. What you are going to hear may include the following:

"I left school for just a semester because I wanted to save money and come back."

"I dropped to part-time so that I could work 40 hours a week and make more money."

"I was pregnant, so I went home for a while and I was going to come back after having the baby."

The list goes on and on. What you might have noticed in this list is that *everyone planned to come back.* Most of those who drop out of college don't plan to stay out, they expect to come back. At the age of 20 or 21, it's easy to think that the opportunities you have today are going to be there for you tomorrow and forever. What they do not realize (that you and I realize) is that the window of opportunity closes just a little bit with each passing day. That energetic 20 year old eventually turns into a tired 35 year old, and then an even more exhausted 50 year old. We all get older and look back at some parts of our lives with tremendous regret. It's sad, but true.

Prepare your child for college, let them meet a "Halfling". Hopefully, they will come to the conclusions you need them to reach. It is this kind of wisdom that helps us to avoid temptation.

Teach them how to respond to failure and disappointment

We all have different reactions to disappointment and failure. Some of us work harder, some of us give up. Disillusionment can cause people to change their religion, switch majors, or give up on their dreams. The sad thing about youth is that many of us remember working toward our ambitions with an unhealthy idealism, one where we truly felt that things were going to go exactly as we envisioned them. Then, when things are tougher than we expect, it shocks us.

I recall seeing many Engineering majors every year (for example) who go through the disillusionment process. They get to college, ready to tear down the walls and become the great engineers they've expected themselves to become. Then, there is the first killer Calculus class. That is when you see students question everything in which they believe. They wonder why they ever chose engineering in the first place, and seek out any major that is as far away from Math as they can possibly find. It's sad to see a promising Engineer spending all his/her time studying Social Work or Chinese Philosophy.

You should talk to your child about the disappointments that are sure to come. They should have full knowledge that things are going to be tough. They should also understand that struggle does not imply that they are not qualified, it only means that they've got some things on which they must improve.

Make them pay something toward their education

When I was a kid, my mother did something that I thought was horribly mean. She made me pay rent every month. I hated it, and sometimes I admit I even hated her. The audacity of parents who have no problem making the mortgage every month forcing their teenage son to pay part of the rent!

Years later, as I look back on my mother's choice, I realize that (in her sick little way), she was teaching me a lesson. She was teaching me to appreciate what I had, and the value of being responsible. These lessons continued into college, as she almost never paid for anything by herself. I was always forced to contribute. This was in contrast to many of my friends, who would get new cars from their parents that they would "total", or have money sent in the mail that they would then use to buy beer for all of their friends.

If you make your child contribute to the cost of their education, the amount of the contribution can be symbolic more than anything. If the tuition is $30,000 per year, and they only pay $1,000, that is enough to make them feel the burn a bit and manage their money a little bit better. You will find that when the child contributes to the cost of their education, they have a better understanding of its inherent value. They will be more motivated, more responsible, and more understanding of what you are going through to get them there.

I

Is Your Child
an Athlete?

"Nobody knew that I couldn't read until after I had graduated." – former college basketball star

An athletic scholarship can be a wonderful thing. I once wished that I could get a track scholarship to college. It was more important to me than anything else in the world. I would train in the morning, after school and again at home at night. I was in great shape, but I didn't have the physical gifts necessary to be the athlete I had hoped to become. While I was incredibly disappointed about not being able to play sports, I soon found out that it was a blessing in disguise.

I've seen many students who've played college sports. Many of them had wonderful careers, and some of them went on to the NBA, NFL, WNBA and other professional leagues. At the same time, there were many students who left college feeling bitter, perhaps burned by their coaches whom they felt cared for them. Some of these students were disappointed that they did not have an education. As a professor, I found myself angry for them, given that their universities had made promises that were not kept.

The other thing I've noticed about athletes on campus is that they are forced to mature faster than other students. They have more demands on their time, so not managing time early in their career can lead to dire consequences. They may find themselves getting up early in the morning and practicing until late in the afternoon. After working hard all day on the field and in the classroom, who feels like doing anything other than sleeping? I *certainly* know that doing homework is not going to be very high on anyone's list, that's for *darn sure!*

I admit that I am sometimes disappointed with collegiate athletics. In some ways, they remind me of the military: convincing naïve young people to do things that many of the older administrators would not do. The athletes risk life and limb on the field, but lose their NCAA eligibility if their coach buys them a bologna sandwich or gives them $5 for a movie ticket. At the same time, the coach may have just signed a multimillion dollar contract to go with his expensive mansion and private plane. I am not sure, but this doesn't seem to be the American way, since I was brought up to believe that people should be compensated fairly for work that they do.

Based on my experience, I will give you some inside scoops of things that I believe to be true about college athletics. You may want to have a conversation with your child about these issues, and at least make sure that they are in a position more likely to lead to success at the collegiate level, rather than failure.

The love that the university shows your child is probably fleeting

The story is no different from a guy attempting to court a woman to get her to sleep with him. The recruiter comes into your child's home, explaining to the both of you how his athletes are his family and your son is the greatest athlete since Jesus Christ. It's all the same, and they give the speech to thousands of kids every year.

This doesn't mean that your child is not a great athlete. But the reality is that the coaches are simply doing what they have to do to make your child another option in their athletic arsenal. If your child doesn't perform on the court or on the field, their future could be in jeopardy.

I had a student once that was potentially on track to be the first athlete in his school's history to spend less than 3 years in college before going to the NFL. He was a great player. He was also a smart player. He was an Engineering major with a solid grade point average. He planned to open his own company after playing professional football. But after his second year in college, he found himself in the hospital with a shattered bone in his arm. Although he wanted to come back, he was told by doctors that he could never play football again.

Now faced with a liability on their hands, the coaches then tried to figure out how to get rid of the student. He was a lame duck to them, someone who simply took up a scholarship from another player they could have on the field. Eventually, the coaches found a reason to get rid of him. He dropped out of college the following semester.

The key thing to learn from this story is that you should take the coach's words with a grain of salt. They are going to say whatever they need to say in order to get you to sign on the dotted line. But the way they feel about your child is usually going to depend on how effective that child is at helping the coach to keep their job.

Check the deal that you are offered, and ask them what happens to your child in the event that they cannot play sports anymore. Get it in writing, because someone can always deny having made a promise to you. If they say that they can't put it in writing, remember that everything is negotiable if they want your child bad enough. If they are not willing to do this, then find a school that will.

Academic scholarships are almost always better than athletic ones

I was "forced" to take a partial academic scholarship rather than the athletic one that I really wanted. I soon became the envy of my athletic friends, who found themselves in practice all the time and on the road even more. They were missing classes and always exhausted while the rest of us were having a great time.

Your child may find that the rigors of college athletics are too much to bear. If this is the case, they are better off if they are not beholden to an athletic scholarship. Many scholarships have clauses that simply state that if your child quits the team, they are going to lose their financial aid. Of course you do not want this to happen. The best way to prepare your child for this possibility is to convince them to take an academic scholarship and then try walking onto the athletic team. That way, they are not controlled by the NCAA. The sports teams should have control of your child on the field, but your child should have freedom when they are off.

Check the graduation rates of the schools you are considering

Find out if your school is getting athletes out the door with paper diplomas, or if they are getting sent away with eviction notices. There is a difference. Many major universities with amazing athletic programs have *horrible* graduation rates. This is again, part of the hypocrisy of the NCAA, which claims to put academics first, except for when the multi-billion dollar television contracts roll up. You do not want your child to be a victim of their greed.

Don't just ask the school what their graduation record is, check an objective source. That might mean going to major magazines, doing a search on the Internet (i.e. going to www.google.com and typing "university graduation rates"), or just asking different people who are familiar with college sports teams about the graduation rates of various universities. The reason that it is important to check multiple sources is because a) people lie and you will probably be lied to at some point if your child is talented enough, and b) there are different measures for graduation rates. For example, a school might measure graduation rates by how many students *eventually* get their degree. That means that the student gets added to the total even if they graduate at 40 years old from another university. Some universities might only count the graduation rates from many years ago, claiming that the past 8 years is not enough time to see what happens to all of their students. But if the students used in their survey all went to school under a previous coach, these numbers might not mean anything. Getting an assessment from multiple sources can help you come to your own conclusions.

Make sure that your child chooses their own major

I once had a student that was a star of the basketball team. Before the class began for the semester, I received an email from one of the coaches, telling me that "John will not be in class this week because he has a game in Nebraska". I felt bad for John for two reasons: 1) the game wasn't until 3 days after the class, but apparently the basketball team decided to leave several days early, and 2) missing the first class or two in my courses gets you off on the wrong foot. The class I was teaching was for seniors and extremely difficult. John's absence was setting him up for failure.

A few days later, I realized that John still had not come to class. The class had met 3 times, but I had yet to meet John. I then received another email, not from John, but from some anonymous coach. The email said "John missed a second class because he had to attend an honorary luncheon."

I will admit that I was not as understanding the second time around. First, I wondered why in the world going to lunch was more important than coming to class. "Perhaps he could have bought a sandwich with him?" I thought to myself. More seriously, I wondered if he or his coaches cared that he was going to have a hard time in my class when he came back. I was also concerned because of the fact that John himself was not sending me these emails. Instead, I was getting these messages from someone else. I was nice, but many professors would have taken this personally.

After missing the first 4 classes or so, I finally get the chance to meet John. He is a nice kid, and a smart kid, smarter than his grade would eventually show. He also told me that he loved Finance. He said that he would have majored in it had his coaches not told him that he could not major in Finance because it interfered with his football schedule.

`The story I told you about John is quite typical of college athletes. Collegiate athletics is not amateur sports, it exhibits many of the characteristics of professional sports. I've heard many coaches over the years say "I expect my young men to be professionals." The sad thing is that they are not professionals, for they are not being paid for their work. They are kids. Like kids, I've seen many of them make horrible mistakes.

When your child gets into college sports, there is some chance that they will have a coach that works to influence their choice of major. They may have very good reasons for telling your child to choose a major that is easier. For example, Engineering is tough for those who do not play sports, let alone those with 40 or 50 hour per week sports schedules. If your child is truly committed to a particular major, you may want to make sure that they attend a university that is going to support their choice of major and not try to get them to change their mind.

Get in touch with an ex-athlete or two

Before your child chooses a particular university, they should speak to as many people as they can about life "after the honeymoon". That means you may want to read up on the coach that the child is going to be playing for and also talk to ex-athletes. Most universities are like anyone else trying to sell something to you, they are going to put their best foot forward. The disgruntled ex-athlete is *not* the one that the coach is going to allow to talk to your son or daughter.

You may want to make an unofficial visit to the university and spend time talking with athletes in the current system that are unsupervised. They may also be able to help you contact ex-athletes after graduation. The key idea is that you should talk to as many people as you can to find out what life will be like playing for the coach that is trying to recruit your child.

Prepare them for the real world

As you probably know already, athletes receive a great deal of adulation, love and respect from others very early in their lives. This can be a wonderful and intoxicating kind of thing. The saddest thing in the world, however, is to see an ex-athlete that is no longer the popular person he once was. It can be sad if that person has not developed themselves outside their sport. The loss of fame and respect can lead to intense depression and self-esteem issues as the athlete adjusts to life as a fast food worker, or something else they may be doing if they did not take advantage of their educational opportunity.

On the other hand, there are ex-athletes who simply saw sports as a channel for them to better themselves educationally. They do not define themselves by their sports, and instead, they see themselves as complete people both on and off the court. These are the individuals that are happiest in the long run.

I went to school with a great athlete. He was a star basketball player, and everyone knew that he was going to play college sports one day. But his father, knowing of his son's talent, made sure that his son was just as good in the classroom as he was on the court. So, although his son received all the respect of a great athlete, he also dominated in advanced academic courses. Eventually, his son earned a college degree and went on to earn hundreds of millions of dollars in the NBA. What I found ironic about his success was that even in high school, there were better athletes around him who did not make the correct life choices. Now, many of those guys are back at home, right where they started, while he is on national television every week.

Prepare your child to make the right life choices. Force them to realize that if you can learn the difficult and complex plays on the football field, you can also learn to do math. A student should not turn their "effort button" off when they walk off the field. They should be a champion in everything they attempt to do.

The 411

Lists of things that every parent should remember when sending their child to college

What professors want from students

1) To be prepared for class

Sounds simple, but most students are not prepared for class. Preparation solves 60% of all class related problems.

2) To do what we tell them to do (which usually isn't that much).

Following directions is a huge problem for college students. Can you get away with this on the job?

3) To be prepared in advance when you come to see us in our office.

This is a matter of respect. I value my time, so I don't enjoy it being wasted by a student who didn't pay attention when I taught everything the first time. Struggling is understood, but we can tell which students are expecting us to bail them out.

4) To come see us at times *other* than the week before the exam.

My office stays empty for most of the month. Then when the test gets here, you would think I was President of the United States!

5) To read all assignments that we give you

Sounds simple. Most students don't do it. If your child does this, they are going to be well ahead of the game.

6) To show up to class

Missing class is the quickest way to fail. It doesn't matter if we know the student is not there. We can usually tell when you come to class and ask us about something that everyone else in the room already knows. Students who miss class do not get the benefit of the doubt when final grades are given.

7) To not expect us to catch you up if you miss class.

I don't get mad when students miss my class. But I don't feel that it is my job to catch them up if they've chosen to be irresponsible. A student that is adult enough to miss class is adult enough to find out what they missed. A professor with 200 students does not have time to teach the material over and over again.

8) To take responsibility for your own actions.

A lack of personal responsibility is one of the biggest immaturity issues with college students. Kids that come from privileged backgrounds have this problem the worst. This skewed perception does not help them when they go into the real world.

9) To keep us in the loop when things go wrong for you.

I've had students who've gone through terrible things, but because they take personal responsibility too far, they don't tell me what is going on. I encourage students to let the professor know what is going on in their lives if they feel that the information is crucial. While the professor may not be completely sympathetic, there are issues that warrant special consideration.

10) Results, not excuses.

There is a line between excuses that are legitimate and those that are just BS. "I overslept because I partied all weekend" is not acceptable, and neither is it ok to provide an excuse for poor performance after the fact. If you look at #9 (above), I am saying that extenuating issues should be communicated with the professor. But the same old lame excuses from the same students over and over doesn't cut it. While tough circumstances may warrant consideration, the rule of thumb is that a student shouldn't have more than one strong excuse per year (i.e. getting sick, major family or personal problems, etc.). If they have an emergency every month, then there is a problem.

What professors want from parents

1) To teach your children personal responsibility

Many students are simply apples that have fallen from their parents' tree. When you send your child to college, don't send them to be a terror for everyone they deal with. I am reminded of a couple of students that none of the faculty would deal with because they always had a complaint and felt that everything was owed to them. You don't want your child to be that person.

2) To teach your kids to work hard. Help them to learn that a little hard work is not such a bad thing.

Most college students do not yet know how to work hard. The ones who are taught this value from their parents are ahead of the other students.

3) To help them value their educational opportunities

Sometimes we don't appreciate something until it's gone. College is not one of those things you want to lose in order to see that it has value.

4) To monitor their study and personal habits.

You should make sure that your child is studying and living the right kind of life when they are away at campus. It is tough to keep up with everything, but you can certainly ask questions.

5) To trust us to educate your children – complaints may be necessary, but usually we are trying to do the right thing.

No professor likes the complaining parent. It puts a nasty stigma on your child. Complain if necessary, but not all the time.

6) If there is a dispute, don't be a superhero. Counsel the child, but don't do the job for them.

You want to avoid the annoying parent phone calls. This only tells us that your child is too immature to handle their own issues. Therefore, they receive the spoiled brat label.

7) Make sure your child understands that college is not like high school (things are not going to be spoon fed).

While most college professors care about their students, it is difficult to play parent to hundreds of people. Students have to understand that the nurturing they had in high school disappears when you enter into adulthood.

8) Give your child a sense of purpose as they head to college – make sure that they know WHY they are there in the first place. You can start by letting them make some of their own decisions.

Kids with no purpose shoot for nothing. Help them obtain a sense of purpose, but do not give it to them. If they are involved in the process of setting personal goals, they are more likely to work hard to achieve them.

Mistakes that parents make when dealing with their college-age children

1) Giving money and expecting nothing in return.

If that is not how the real world works, then that is not how things should work in your household. Even if a student is making good grades, pouring money on them with no additional work required only leads them to that much more disappointment when they reach the real world.

2) *Expecting* their kids to be irresponsible.

When your child does something that makes no sense, don't just accept it as part of going to college. There are many students who go to college and keep their fun in moderation. You should expect no different from your child. Also, when they are not responsible either financially or in the classroom, this is not something that you should accept.

3) Taking out loans for their children and then repaying them.

If you are trying to prepare for retirement, there is no reason for you to carry this extra burden, particularly since the person you are carrying it for may eventually make as much money as you do.

4) Paying for every single expense the child has when going off to college

Who wrote the rule that says parents should pay for all of their child's expenses? Doesn't that make your child a welfare recipient?

5) Not monitoring their academic performance regularly during the semester

A student may demand the respect of an adult, but does an adult have someone else paying all the bills? The university may not give you the right to ask them directly about your child's grades, but there is no reason that you can't ask the child directly.

6) Not keeping up with their child's habits.

Your child's life can spin out of control pretty fast. Try to find creative ways to keep up with what they are doing with their time.

7) Not discussing the things that their child is going to experience when they get to college.

Some parents have a hard time talking to their kids about real life. But I am sure you would prefer to have them learn the information from you rather than hearing it from someone else. Also, real life is not going to hold any punches, so you shouldn't either.

8) Not making sure that their child has taken a college-prep curriculum

Just because your child has good grades, that doesn't mean they are actually learning something. Make sure they are taking classes in high school that are going to prepare them for college.

9) Always siding with their child on every issue when dealing with a professor.

If your child has a dispute with a professor, it is not always the professor's fault. Investigate the issue, but don't always stand by your child's story when they have an excuse for failure. It will catch up with them eventually.

10) Not encouraging your child to pursue higher education or graduate school.

After your child leaves high school, they should go to college. After your child leaves college, they should go to graduate school. There is nothing more to say than that.

11) Letting kids move back home when things don't work out.

If you let them move back in, you should be prepared to take care of them for another decade. Don't start that bad habit, for a child that is handed a pair of crutches at an early age is tempted to use them for good.

12) Not encouraging the kid to do something with their summer.

The summers are not for lounging around doing nothing. They are for building a future. The child can have fun during the summer, but they should be doing something constructive, like an internship or going to summer school full time. This time should NOT be wasted.

13) Forcing their children into a major they hate, or allowing them to choose a major that is not good for them.

I have seen students that are forced to choose a major by their parents. They hate what they do, and their parents' money is wasted. I have also seen students that choose a major solely based on what they like to do. They are then shocked to find out that they have committed themselves to a life of poverty. Don't let your child make this mistake.

14) Making sure that they have to save their child from every silly thing that they do.

Your child's mistakes belong to them. You are not their personal parachute.

The inside scoop on what goes on in college

1) Venereal disease rates on college campuses are much higher than those of the general population.

You have thousands of horny, energetic people all cooped up together with nothing to do. What do YOU think is going to happen?

2) Kids who get lots of money from their parents tend to be the laziest.

There is a direct connection between how much a student has to do on their own and how lazy they are. The students with everything handed to them tend to be the weakest mentally.

3) There is a lot of terrible crime that happens on college campuses. The universities just don't necessarily want you to know that.

If you thought your child would be in danger on a given campus, would you send them? Universities know this. Check the crime statistics for the area that the university is in, as well as the campus itself. Some universities are honest about their reporting, but some may understate the numbers to keep their enrollment high.

4) Gambling and videogame addictions are almost as strong and destructive as drug and alcohol addictions.

I have seen literal video game zombies on campus. There are people that play these games for 15 or 16 hour straight, doing no studying in between. It can interrupt a student's studying as much, or more than a full time job. Leave the Xbox and Play Station at home.

5) Most students change their major several times during their college career.

If your child is undecided when they arrive, don't hound them for it. They are probably going to change their mind anyway. Just remind them that searching for a major is something that should be done right away.

6) In most college majors, it should only take 4 years to graduate if you are focused and know what you need to do.

If your child tries to tell you that everybody takes 5 or 6 years, you don't have to accept this. Also, universities are going to say this because they want another year of tuition money. If you demand that your child get out of college in 4 years, you can usually do it.

7) There are far more people in the world who have completed one or two years of college than there are who've actually gotten a degree.

Getting into college is not the same as graduating. Many people have left halfway in the process. Your child should be aware of this so that they can keep their focus.

8) Most students that flunk out of college do so for reasons that have nothing to do with academics.

Most students suffer academically because they have become distracted. If your child takes care of business first, they can have all the fun they want to have.

9) There is no such thing as college material. Your high school counselor may be wrong.

The phrase "college material" was essentially invented so that our society would have enough people to wash windows and clean the streets. I don't know about you, but I want my child to have a better life than that.

10) The more expensive universities are not necessarily better than those that cost less money.

It's not as much about where you go to school as it is about how well you do while you are there. I am still trying to figure out why people spend 30k per year to go to college when they really don't have to and can't afford the cost.

11) Many students who did extremely well in high school are almost as likely as other students to struggle and even flunk out in college.

I don't care what your child's grade point average was in high school. The entire ball game has changed. I have seen just as many "top" students drop out of college as average ones. What matters is your child's mentality when they arrive on campus, nothing more

What you might want to know about professors and the classroom

1) Professors are not as all-powerful as you might think.

Professors are like judges in the courtroom. You should respect their authority, but they can't do whatever they want. There are ways that you can counter what the professor has done if they have indeed done something unethical.

2) At many universities, complaining and lazy students can reduce the quality of education

Professors are human too. If they see that many of the students are complaining and lazy (i.e. Screwing up their teaching evaluations), there is a strong temptation for them to "dumb down" the class so that there isn't as much complaining. So, sometimes at private universities, where there are many spoiled students, the kids get the worst education. Professors don't like complaints, since it makes them look bad to the dean. It takes a special person to force you to do something that is good for you when you are attacking them constantly for making you do it. Most professors will not lose their job to force students to learn things they do not want to learn.

3) Most students don't read the chapter to be covered in class until after the class, even though the professor tells them to.

The student who actually reads everything in advance is going to be noticed by the professor.

4) Not all professors are created equal, some have more power than others.

There are adjuncts, instructors, T.A.s, assistants, associates and full professors. The Adjuncts, T.A.s and instructors do not have a lot of power, and are afraid of looking bad to their department. The Assistants, Associates and Full Professors all have PhDs. The Assistants, however, do not yet have tenure. They are sort of like someone that is engaged to the university, but not yet married. The Associates have tenure, but they will probably never be Full Professors. Full Professors have usually been around a long time and developed a national reputation. Beware of whom you are dealing with so that you know how to approach potential problems with the university.

5) Most college courses give you a "B" just for doing what you are supposed to do.

If you get an "A" or a "C", you've done something extraordinary to make this happen. Ivy league and private schools tend to have even more inflated grades than state universities, since student complaints can cause professors to make their courses easier.

6) Most professors don't care what the student did or did not achieve in high school.

When you come into my class, all that matters to me is what you do right then. I don't care how many awards you won during your senior year. I also don't care if you were a bad student. If you work hard in my class, you are going to be rewarded. Also, a very weak argument for a student that has done poorly would be "But I get good grades in all my other classes." I honestly don't care what you have done in your other classes. The slate is clean when you deal with me.

7) Most courses are not all that demanding, since professors know that half the students aren't going to do the work anyway.

My class could and should be much harder than it is. But since I know that half the students aren't going to remember even the most basic information from the last course, I am forced to rehash it. Also, the bad students slow down the pace. If I were to force the pace more, I would have lots of complaints from the dean. It's a sticky situation, but one that a hard working student can use to their advantage.

8) The syllabus tells you everything you need for the entire semester, so someone can get as far ahead in class as they want.

College provides the chance to plan the entire semester. A smart student is one that makes their calendar early so that nothing creeps up on them. The syllabus gives them an advantage that they should utilize when making long term plans.

What Parents of collegiate athletes need to ponder

1) If your child plays basketball or football, the NCAA is using your child. At least get something in return.

It is sad to see that while players earn billions for their universities, they only receive measly scholarships in return. What is worse is that many players walk away without even receiving the education they were promised. Make sure your child is not in the group of the scorned.

2) They don't tend to care if you graduate

Nearly half of all basketball and football players at the collegiate level do not graduate[vii]. The numbers are really bad at many of the top 20 sports programs in this country. So, while the schools are very proficient at making sure that they are guaranteed their billions of dollars every year, guaranteeing a college diploma is not considered possible. It's funny how the things that matter to us most are always taken care of first.

3) In many universities, academics are second to sports in general.

I recall once seeing a top athlete taken up on academic misconduct charges. The panel had 4 faculty and 3 students. All students were clearly convinced that he had plagiarized when it was clear that he could only read on a second grade level. But guess what? The students were outvoted by the faculty, who knew their jobs were going to be gone if they were to damage the athletics program.

4) They don't love your child the way they say they do.

Athletes have value to most coaches as long as they are athletic. Once they can't play anymore, they become dead weight. It is important that you protect your child from this possibility, since many athletes end their careers early. This is especially true in football, where injuries occur quite easily.

5) An academic scholarship is better than an athletic one.

If you are getting your financial aid from someplace else, that is one less thing your coach can hold over your head. This can reduce the pressure on the student athlete quite a bit.

6) Many schools will use sex and parties to lure your child

The University of Colorado is just one example of a case in which the athletics program was shown to use unethical tactics to recruit athletes. You may find that your child is being introduced to older strippers or unseemly people on their recruiting trips. You may want to watch out for this kind of thing.

7) If your child gets into trouble, the "surrogate parents" may suddenly forget that you are related.

Many of us have heard a coach say "He is like a son to me". That sounds wonderful when they say it, but the reality is that when most athletes get into serious trouble, the sports authorities do their best to disassociate from that person. This is part of self-preservation and saving the athletic program. An unsuspecting 18 year old may not be aware of exactly how fragile this relationship is.

8) Force your child to learn their academic program so that they know what classes they need to take.

If you are contributing to the cost, make sure that you approve of their class schedule before they sign up for it. While not true for all coaches and programs, I have seen coaches make schedules with the simple goal of setting up the easiest schedule possible that won't interfere with practice and will allow the student to remain eligible to play sports. That is why all the football players end up clumped in the underwater pottery class.

What parents of minority students need to know

1) "Diversity" is only a buzzword on most college campuses.

Most universities don't work very hard to make their campuses diverse, particularly at the faculty level. If they truly wanted diversity, they would have had it by now.

2) Racist incidents do occur on college campuses all the time

As an undergraduate resident advisor, I recall seeing the word "Nigger" on the nice bulletin board I had set up for my residents. This is just one of many incidents I had to deal with over the years. The incidents continue, and some of them are very serious. I also recall an incident occurring in which several students dropped out of school after being threatened, one was dead, and another was in critical condition. Things can get pretty serious on campus.

3) Minority student graduation rates tend to be very low on many campuses.

I am not going to speculate on exactly why this happens, but be prepared for the fact that your child may be dealing with barriers that are slightly higher than those of other students. In the end, you should be prepared to ensure that your child is ready to fight the barriers and overcome them.

4) Many schools will lump all minorities together to make their numbers look larger than they actually are.

When they say that their campus is 10% minority, find out what composition they are referring to. If you are concerned about African-Americans, Native Americans or Hispanics, the numbers may be actually much lower than that.

5) Black professors can be used as bait to pull in minorities and athletes, but the professors may be temporary

*Remember: assistant professors are not tenured. That means that while the university may show off the professor to get your child to come to the university, the person may actually be out the door. Many academic departments have **Never** given tenure to an underrepresented minority, my own included.*

6) Prepare your child for the fact that they may not have hardly anyone around that looks like them.

Some kids can only conceptualize what it would be like to attend a university that is 95% white. It is only when they get there that they feel the reality. You should visit the campus first so that your child knows what they are getting themselves into.

My last few pieces of advice

1) If your child pledges a frat or sorority do not let them pledge during their freshman year. You might also make them pay for it.

Most campuses don't allow students to pledge during their Freshman year. If your campus does, do not allow your child to do it. Also, make them pay their own fraternity and sorority dues to ensure that this is what they want to do. While pledging has its benefits, I have seen the process cause just as many problems. I am not here to tell your child if they should pledge, I am just saying that you should make sure that they do it the right way.

2) Don't get your child a car or an apartment until after their sophomore year.

Cars and apartments are major distractions. They have the rest of their lives to live by themselves and drive their car, give them time to be kids first.

3) Let them pay the price for some of their mistakes.

Remember: if they don't experience the pain, then they will always miss the gain.

4) Force the child to get a job – this will teach them to manage their time.

It is hard to manage time effectively if you've got a ton of it. But when the time is constrained, this makes the person more time conscious. Don't let your child have a lot of free time, it does them no good.

5) Understand that they are going to make mistakes, accept that and move on.

Encourage and support your child, but do not badger them to death when they screw up. That is going to happen. You should help them to grow from their mistakes.

6) Do not let them get away with lazy behavior.

Many college students are lazy. If they are lazy, make sure that they pay the price for their shiftlessness. Do not support it by cleaning up after them forever.

7) If they start to slip, cut their financial strings one by one.

Losing money is a great motivator. Make sure that there is an effort tied to every reward, this is how you create the right incentives.

8) Do not take out student loans for you child, they can pay some of that money back also.

I've never understood why parents do this. Given that many college students make a lot of money when they graduate, they are certainly capable of paying their own student loans.

Some Collegiate Vices

1) sexual promiscuity/venereal diseases

It's sad, but true. Sex is very natural, but many kids are not educated sexually. Make sure that your child at least knows what they are doing when they start to become sexually active.

2) Gambling

This is one of the best-kept secrets in college. But now that Poker tournaments are on television, you would be amazed at how many students are starting to get into this kind of thing. Try to keep an eye on your child's habits and make sure that this isn't one of them.

3) Drugs

Drugs have been around for a while. Make sure that your child knows the consequences. At that point, the decision is theirs. If you find out that your child is involved in drugs, of course you know that you should help them to seek counseling. There is help right on campus.

4) Alcohol

This is one of the oldest and dumbest traditions of college. I am not sure why people feel that alcohol should be abused on campus, but it happens. Prepare your child to be smart when dealing with this stuff, for it has led to a lot of deaths, rapes, murders and arrests.

5) Laziness/procrastination/cramming

Some laziness and procrastination is natural, but students can be the worst. Teaching your child good study habits before they arrive is the best you can do to combat this problem early in the game.

6) Using the abortion clinic as a birth control pill

Many young girls still do not know that more than one abortion is not healthy. Teach this to your child. Also, make sure that they are not afraid to tell you if they are pregnant. I have seen students literally kill their babies and go to prison because they were so afraid of disappointing their parents. Do not let your child be the next tragedy.

7) Horrible money management and overuse of credit card debt.

Credit problems created in college can exist forever. Have your child learn the value of money management. Also protect them from the credit card hounds that are waiting for them when they get to campus. If they don't listen and get a credit card anyway, DO NOT pay the bill for them, EVER!

8) Video game addictions

Video games are one of the other rising addictions on campuses. Students who spend all their time in front of the TV are not going to get much studying done. Make sure that your child learns the value of balance. Do not let them bring their game consoles to campus unless their grades are good, and if they get themselves into trouble academically because they refuse to listen, let them deal with the drama that comes afterward.

Eight things every parent should do before their child leaves for college

1) Send them with some condoms, lots of them.

Yes, it is hard to think about them using them, but there is a good chance they are. Why is it so hard to talk about sex, when it is the reason that most of us got to this earth in the first place?

2) Force the student to learn their academic program.

Do not accept a "Yeah, duuuuh" approach to college. Your child should know their academic program BEFORE they get there. You should then expect them to tell you what their long-term plan is and how they expect to get out of college within the next 4 years. It is your money and your child, so it is your RIGHT to know.

3) Make your child get a part-time job.

If your child is working, they will manage their time. If they are not, they will waste it. Teach them early about the value of working hard for what they get.

4) Teach them about making a time budget.

Many students do not know how to manage their time. It is up to their parents to show them how. The first step is to make them aware of exactly how many hours per week they have at their disposal, then show them what to do with that time.

5) Make sure that your daughter is taken care of in the birth control category.

Explain to her the importance of taking the pills every day if she chooses to use them. You may also want to talk to her about female condoms and the importance of being mature with her sexuality. I am not sure about asking her to abstain, since that can be a double-edged sword. This may worsen her behavior in the event that she chooses not to abstain. I recommend giving the information on an "in case you need it" basis, without judging her as a person.

6) Do a "reality check" as you show them the consequences of not making the right choices.

Remember the reality check I mentioned earlier in the book? I recommend that you do this with your child before they head to college. Show them real life examples of what can happen if they choose not to use their educational opportunities.

7) Have them download the syllabus for every class they are taking and go over their schedule carefully.

The professor's syllabus is usually on the Internet weeks in advance. The smart students are the one who have this information early. There is no law against starting to study early.

8) Get the child on campus 3 weeks ahead of time, if you can, or preferably at the start of the summer.

Summer school right before the freshman year is one of the best ways to get used to the campus environment. The student can learn their way around before everyone else gets there, and it gives them a chance to learn how things work.

About The Author

Dr. Boyce D. Watkins earned BA and BS degrees from The University of Kentucky with a nearly perfect GPA and a triple major in Finance, Economics and Business Management. In college, he was selected as the Wall Street Journal Outstanding Graduating Senior in Finance, Freshman of the Year, and the Lyman T. Johnson Outstanding Graduating Senior. He then earned a Masters Degree in Mathematical Statistics from The University of Kentucky and a PhD in Finance from The Ohio State University. He now teaches Finance at Syracuse University, where he is the first African-American faculty member in the history of the Department of Finance. Of nearly 4,000 Finance Faculty in the U.S., Dr. Watkins is one of only 5 African-Americans teaching at a top 50-business school, and the only African-American to earn a PhD in Finance during the year 2002 . He is the author of *Everything You Ever Wanted to Know About College – A Guide for Minority Students* and *Quick and Dirty Secrets of College Success – A Professor Tells it All.* He is also the National Director of the *Step up and Go to College Tour*, which travels to 18 – 20 cities around the US to speak to youth and parents on college empowerment.

Order Form

To order copies of books, please use the order form on this page. The form can be mailed to:

The Blue Boy Publishing Co.
PO Box 691
Camillus, NY. 13031 – 0691

You can also fax the form to: (866) 436-5418
Please call (315) 487-1176 for questions

Everything You Ever Wanted to Know About College
Number of copies _____   x $18 = _____

Quick and Dirty Secrets of College Success
Number of copies _____ x $15 = _____

Total cost of books ordered _____

Please send a check or money order, along with this order form, for the total cost of books ordered to the address listed above.

You can also email questions to: info@boycewatkins.com and visit www.boycewatkins.com for information about going to college or to request Dr. Watkins as a speaker.

[i] Ken Winters, "Gambling and College Students", Gambling Problems Resource Center

[ii] ibid

[iii] Center for Disease Control, 1995, College Health Risk Behavior Survey

[iv] ibid

[v] Society of Adolescent Medicine survey

[vi] *The Real Facts about College, 2004*

[vii] The Chronicle of Higher Education, 2002

Printed in the United States
21052LVS00005B/196-240